The Changing
Face of
COLCHESTER

Patrick Denney

The Changing
Face of
COLCHESTER

Patrick Denney

breedon **books**
PUBLISHING

First published in Great Britain in 2002 by
The Breedon Books Publishing Company Limited
Breedon House, 3 The Parker Centre,
Derby, DE21 4SZ.

Dedication
For Stephen & Beverly and Paul & Genevieve

ISBN 1 85983 301 2

Printed and bound by Butler & Tanner, Frome, Somerset, England.

Cover printing by Lawrence-Allen Colour Printers,
Weston-super-Mare, Somerset.

Contents

Acknowledgements

I owe a debt of gratitude to many people who have assisted in the production of this book either by making available treasured archive photographs, or by providing me with information for use in the text. I would, however, like to single out the following individuals for a special mention as their overall help and assistance has been invaluable.

Firstly, I would like to make particular mention of the contribution made by Marcel Glover who was responsible for producing many of the images used in the book, particularly the modern day photographs which have mainly been used for comparative purposes.

I am also greatly indebted to Peter Berridge (general manager) and Tom Hodgson (curator of social history) from the Museum Resource Centre for allowing me access to the vast photographic collection in their keeping, and for their kind permission for the photographs chosen to be copied and reproduced.

I would also like to thank Mark Davies for allowing an abridged version of his unpublished *Chronology of Colchester* to be included in the book.

Finally, I would to thank the following organisations and individuals for their various contributions towards the book's publication:

David Appleton, Joan Barritt, Andrew Barker, Jean Barnett, Luke Berriman, Jean Blowers, Mick Brown, John Collins, Philip Crummy, Christine Denney, Len and Nora Drinkell, Jill and Mervyn Fairweather, Nora Frost, Alan Garnett, Geoffrey Gunton, Frances Harwood, Andrea Hitchcock, Mike Hogg, Christine Johns, Dave Kennedy, Jim Lee, Carol Lyon, Ian McMeekan, Margaret Madden, Dennis Marchant, Amanda Murphy, Russell Newman, Les Nunn, Michael Pearce, Tony Petter, Andrew Phillips, Brian and Cynthia Pierpoint, Bernard Polley, Gill and David Poppleton, Alan Rayner, Michael and Janet Read, Jim Robinson, Bob Russell, Sharon Sciachettano, Reg Shelley, Martin Sibley, Roger Smith, David Snow, Frank Thompson, Bill Tucker, Clive Waddington, Diana Wadley and Paul Wendon.

Anglian Water Services Ltd, Benham & Co Ltd, Brackett Green Ltd, Colchester Archaeological Trust, Colchester Bowling Club, Colchester Fire Brigade, Paxman Diesels, Stanway Traffic Police, Tempest Ltd, Woods Air Movement Ltd, North County Primary School, Old Heath Community Primary School, St Helena School and St John's Green Primary School.

If I have made any omissions, it is with regret and is no way intentional.

Historical Introduction

Colchester is Britain's oldest recorded town and is blessed with a rich and varied historical past stretching back over 2,000 years. Originally known as Camulodunum, after the war-god Camulos, the settlement was the stronghold of the Trinovantes, which under the rule of the celebrated King Cunobelin (Shakespeare's Cymbeline), became the 'capital' of Iron Age Britain. The site was also chosen by the Romans to erect their first legionary fortress and colonia (city), and later, following the death of Emperor Claudius in AD 54, for the building of a massive Roman temple, the first of its kind in Britain. The stone base or foundation podium of the temple still survives beneath the remains of the Norman castle, itself a building that survives as a major visitor attraction.

In AD 61 following the death of her husband Prasutagus of the Iceni tribe, Queen Boudicca, after being beaten by the Romans and seeing her daughters raped, led an armed revolt against their Roman conquerors. After amassing a huge force of native Britons drawn from both the Iceni and neighbouring tribes, they marched on the Colonia at Colchester which they subsequently overran and destroyed by fire. In fact, it would appear from the archaeological record that the town may have been systematically destroyed, building by building, reducing everything to ashes. The Roman colonists decided to seek refuge inside the mighty temple, hoping against hope that reinforcements would be sent to save them. After a siege lasting just two days the roof was finally set on fire and those inside killed. The marauding mob then marched on London and St Albans both of which suffered a similar fate.

The town was subsequently rebuilt and enclosed within a massive defensive wall, much of which still survives in modern Colchester. The town would doubtless have been modelled on existing Roman settlements of the period and would have included such features as a forum, bath house, basilica and theatre. In fact, of the four Roman theatres thus far discovered in Britain, two are to be found in Colchester, both of which would have been capable of seating upwards of 3,000 people. The population of Roman Colchester during this period may well have risen to as high as 10,000, a figure not again seen until the 18th century.

Following the break up of the Roman Empire in the early 5th century, Colchester was inhabited by various Saxons and Danish invaders, although little is known of the fortunes of the town during this period. The *Anglo-Saxon Chronicle* informs us that by the early 10th century the town was being occupied by a Danish garrison who were subsequently routed by King Edward the Elder in 917. In 921 Edward returned to repair and rebuild the town walls. There is no evidence, however, that the town was of any particular importance during

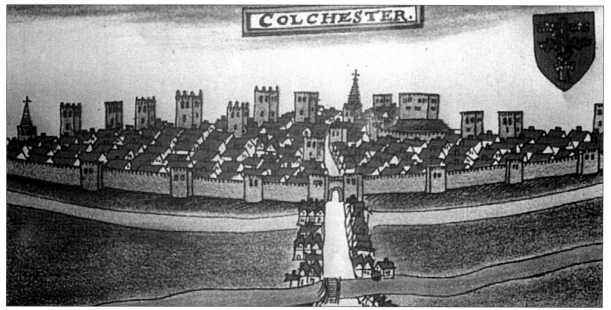

This is probably the earliest known image of Colchester. It dates from the 1580s and shows the town from its eastern prospect looking towards East Hill. The Roman East Gate can be seen straddling the road, either side of which can be seen the town wall. The light coloured band in front of the wall is presumably the town ditch, and in the foreground can be seen a footbridge crossing the River Colne with the old East Mill on the right. Finally, note the castle standing at the top of the hill to the right of the church steeple surrounded by what looks like an earthen embankment and stone curtain wall.

Another early view of Colchester drawn at the time of the visit to England of Cosimo, the Duke of Tuscany, in 1669. This was just over 20 years after the Siege of Colchester and the ruins of St Mary's Church can be seen on the left. Note also what appears to be the castle on the far right, which interestingly shows the building as it would have appeared before it was partially demolished later in the century. Although this is not a totally reliable image, it would appear to portray a building rising to no more than two storeys.

this period, although many of the town's churches were probably founded at this time.

Following the Norman Conquest of 1066, Colchester once again become an important military centre after the town was chosen as the site for building a new castle as part of William's extensive programme of castle building.

The castle, which shares a similar floor plan to that of the Tower of London, was the largest Norman fortress of its kind ever built owing to the fact that it was constructed over and around the base of the Roman temple. The castle served as a royal fortress for several hundred years before being sold off as a redundant building in the 17th century. The new owner was a local ironmonger named John Wheeley who paid just over £100 for the entire edifice, with the sole intent of reducing it to rubble and selling on the resulting stone

The ruins of St Botolph's Priory as seen in a drawing by John Cotman in 1811. Having survived the Dissolution of the Monasteries in 1536 relatively unscathed, at which time the nave and aisles remained in use as a parish church, the building was finally brought to its ruinous condition during the Siege of Colchester in 1648.

and masonry to local builders at a profit. It was during this demolition work that the sand-filled foundations of the Roman temple were discovered and Wheeley set about tunnelling through the 22ft thick foundations and digging out some of the sand. Whether he was simply after the sand or whether he believed that he would find buried treasure is not known. He may simply have intended to undermine the castle walls from below in an attempt to hasten the demolition work. For whatever reason, however, he later decided to abandon the project and what was left of the building was ultimately sold on. By the 1750s, the ruins of the castle had passed into the hands of Charles Gray, a local antiquarian, who set about restoring parts of the building and providing accommodation for his large library. By the 1860s, a small museum had been established in part of the building which, over the years, has developed into what is today a major tourist attraction, housing one of the finest museum collections of Roman antiquities in the country.

Other major buildings erected during the Norman period included St John's Abbey and St Botolph's Priory. The abbey grew into a substantial community of monks who, following the Benedictine order, kept themselves quite separate from the townspeople, refusing to allow them access to worship within the confines of the abbey. This stance ultimately proved to be their downfall at the time of the Dissolution when the abbey was closed down. St Botolph's Priory, on the other hand, which had followed the less resolute Augustinian order which allowed for some degree of public access, was at the time saved from total ruin when the priory church was adopted as the principal place of public worship in the town.

A modern view of the scene similar to that portrayed at the time of Cosimo's visit in 1669. St Mary's Church is partially hidden from view behind the trees to the left of the water tower.

Throughout the Middle Ages, the town remained an important centre of trade and commerce, particularly in relation to the cloth industry during which time a material known as 'Colchester Russett' was produced. During the reign of Queen Elizabeth I the cloth industry took on even greater importance with the arrival in the town of a large number of Flemish refugees who were fleeing from religious persecution in their own countries. The town bailiffs were keen for these refugees to settle here, for they were skilled in the art of producing the so called 'new draperies', a finer lightweight type of cloth known as 'bays and says'. They came to be known as the Dutch Community and were bestowed with numerous privileges, including the right to regulate the entire production of all such cloth produced in the town in their own Dutch Bay Hall. For the next 200 or so years the industry flourished bringing a degree of prosperity and prestige to the town. Unfortunately, because most of the cloth produced was exported to countries in southern Europe, subsequent wars affecting these areas resulted in numerous periods of depression and slump.

Colchester also figured prominently during the English Civil War when the town was besieged by parliamentarian forces for a period of nearly three months. Despite the town being squarely on the side of Parliament during the war years, during the summer of 1648 they found themselves to be unwilling hosts to a large Royalist force which had advanced on the town following an uprising in Kent. When Fairfax's Parliamentarian army arrived shortly afterwards the Royalists found themselves trapped in the town with no means of escape. Refusing to surrender the Royalists took up defensive positions, whilst the Parliamentarians set about encircling the town with a series of forts and earthworks. The resulting siege lasted for 11 weeks during which time the beleaguered people of the town had been reduced to a state of near starvation existing on a diet of horse-flesh, dogs, cats and even rats. In fact, according to one contemporary account, half of the side of a dog was selling on the street for six shillings – approximately £25 in today's terms. When the town finally surrendered, Fairfax ordered the execution of two of the Royalist leaders, and imposed a fine of £14,000 (over a million pounds today), on the town, half of which had to be paid by the Dutch Community. The townspeople were devastated having already suffered a substantial loss of trade and business, as well as the destruction of scores of buildings.

The 17th century was to bring further woe to the town at the time of the Great Plague in 1665–6. Often described as The Great Plague of London, the disease raged with far greater severity in North Essex, and particularly in Colchester where nearly 5,000 people died of the disease during an 18 month period. This amounted to about half of the town's population

A view of Colchester Castle as seen in the early 1820s. The large windows in the front wall and the cupola shaped dome over the Great Stairway, were part of the 18th-century restorations carried out by Charles Gray. Note the small sycamore tree on top of the castle wall which was reputed to have been planted in 1815 to celebrate the Battle of Waterloo. The tree, or indeed a similar one, still survives in the same position to the present day.

making it one of the most destructive outbreaks experienced by any town during the early modern period. Funds raised for the relief of the sufferers in local churches proved inadequate, and additional money was raised from several surrounding towns and villages. At one stage during 1666, collections were even being made in the London churches for the relief of those suffering in Colchester. Ralph Josselin, the vicar of neighbouring Earls Colne, whose personal diary covered period of the Great Plague, made numerous references to the situation in Colchester which included the following entry made on 16 September 1665, 'God good in Colnes preservation, yet Colchester increaseth in illness being spread over the whole town'.

Following the war with Spain in the early 18th century, the fortunes of the local cloth industry again took a nose-dive from which it struggled to recover. In 1728, the Dutch Bay Company was finally wound up and whilst a few baymakers struggled on for a few more decades, the end of the industry was in sight. The final demise of the trade came at the time of the Napoleonic Wars at the end of the century when trade with foreign markets came to a virtual standstill. By 1815 only one baymaker was left trading in the town and he too finally gave up in the 1830s when he sold out to a firm from Yorkshire.

The Napoleonic period did, however, bring some financial advantage to the town in the form of a large barracks which was built on land between what is now Barrack Street and Old Heath Road. The garrison had to be equipped and catered for and local trade benefited for several years, particularly the farming community who found a ready market for the produce. This new found prosperity, however, was short-lived and at the end of the war the barracks were dismantled and sold off. The army did, however, return during the Crimean War at which time a permanent garrison was established which has survived to the present day bringing lasting benefits to the local economy.

Colchester Castle as it appears today.

Milestones of Local History

*c*2000 BC Earliest evidence of human settlement at Colchester from a Neolithic pit found in excavations at Culver Street in 1981.

AD 41 Death of Cunobelin, 'King of the Britons', who from AD 5 had ruled at Camulodunum, defending it with earthen ramparts or dykes and dominating most of S.E. Britain.

43 Roman invasion of Britain and the capture of Camulodunum led in person by the emperor Claudius. Britain's first capital is established at Colchester.

49 Foundation of the Roman colony, *Colonia Claudia*, on the site of the legionary fortress.

60 Rebellion of Boudicca – local Trinovantes join forces with invading Iceni from Norfolk. The Temple of Claudius and the whole Roman colony are totally destroyed.

65-80 Colchester's town walls (the earliest in Britain) are built with Balkerne Gate as main western entrance. An earthen rampart is added internally *c*.100 years later.

79 Pliny the Elder's *Natural History* is published with a passing reference to Camulodunum, which much later gives rise to Colchester's claim to be 'Britain's oldest recorded town'.

248 Birth of Helena, the mother of Constantine, at Drepanum in Bithynia. According to local medieval tradition she was born in Colchester, the daughter of King Coel. She was a Christian and her son was the first Christian Roman emperor.

330 Christian church built in the Roman extramural cemetery at Butt Road; its excavated remains represent the oldest visible Christian building in Britain.

450 Saxons build their huts among the ruins of the Roman town from about this time. The earliest known hut was excavated at Lion Walk in 1972.

917 Edward the Elder expels the Danes, repairs the town walls and establishes the defended settlement or '*burh*' of Colneceaster ('fortress on the Colne' in Old English).

931 Athelstan holds a meeting of his royal council, or '*witan*', in Colchester on 23 March.

1000 Square tower added to the late Saxon church of Holy Trinity. The 10th century or earlier west wall of the nave is the oldest surviving part of Colchester's longest used church.

1076 Colchester Castle begun by Eudo, steward of William I, mostly using recycled Roman bricks and stone. Stone for the dressings was imported from Caen, Barnack and Quarr.

1086 Domesday Book records Colchester as a borough with at least 419 houses, which suggests a population of about 2,500.

1095 Abbey of St John the Baptist is founded by Eudo – planning and marking out on the ground – on 29 August. Building began in 1096, with Eudo laying the first stone.

1100 St Botolph's Priory is established as the first regular house of Augustinian Canons in England by Ernulph, who became the first Prior. It had begun as a Saxon foundation.

1189 Charter granted by Richard I, for a fine of 60 marks, on 6 December at Dover. This is the earliest known borough charter, although it was possibly modified from a previous one.

1215 Colchester Castle is taken by French troops and held for the barons after the signing of Magna Carta at Runnymede on 15 June. King John retakes it nine months later after a siege.

1310 The Court Roll for this year is the earliest surviving Borough record.

1348 Black Death, arriving in winter, lasts until summer 1349. At least a quarter of the town's population died.

1360 A second plague strikes the town, but recovery is again quick and economic prosperity continues to grow as a result of the cloth trade.

1381 Peasants' Revolt, led by Wat Tyler from Kent and John Ball who described himself as 'sometime St Mary priest of York and now of Colchester'.

1413 Charter granted by Henry V on 7 July at a cost of £16. Its finely illuminated initial letter depicts the Borough Arms, with St Helena and Constantine in medieval royal dress.

1428 William Chivelyng, tailor, is convicted of heresy and burnt at the Balkerne Gate on 4 November. For reading Wycliff's English Bible translation he became first Colchester Martyr.

1474 Hythe bridge is rebuilt in stone and timber. Now wide enough for a cart, it replaced the first one, a footbridge, which was permitted by the Corporation in 1407.

1539 St John's Abbey is dissolved; the Abbot, Thomas Marshall or Beche, is attainted for high treason, imprisoned in the Tower and then hanged at Colchester on 1 December.

1558 In the last three years of Queen Mary's reign from 1555 as many as 23 people were burnt at the stake in Colchester, which was described as 'a harbourer of heretics and ever was'.

1561 Queen Elizabeth I spent two or three days in Colchester. In 1579 she stayed at St John's Abbey, home of Sir Thomas Lucas, on her tour of Essex and Suffolk.

1565 The first Dutch refugees arrive – 55 persons in 11 households – fleeing from religious persecution in the Spanish Netherlands. Their new worsted draperies bring prosperity.

1584 Colchester Grammar School is re-founded by a royal charter granted by Queen Elizabeth I on 6 July.

1591 Bourne Mill, one of 9 medieval mills, is rebuilt in its present form by Thomas Lucas as a fishing lodge, using materials from St John's Abbey.

1603 William Gilberd, physician to Elizabeth I and James I, dies and is buried in Holy Trinity church. He discovered electromagnetism, and wrote a treatise *De Magnete* (1600).

1631 Samuel Harsnett or Halsnoth (b.1561), son of a baker in St Botolph's parish, who rose to become Archbishop of York (1628), dies leaving his library to the Borough.

1638 John Wilbye, madrigal composer, who lived for 10 years in Trinity Street in the household of Lady Mary Darcy, Countess Rivers, dies and is buried in Holy Trinity church.

1642 Oliver Cromwell writes a letter to the town on 23 March, requesting troops and provisions to help Parliament's fight against Charles I. A committee is duly appointed.
St John's Abbey, home of the Lucas family since 1548, is attacked and looted by the townspeople as Civil War begins.

1645 Matthew Hopkins, Witch-Finder General, interrogates 15-year-old Rebecca West at the Castle, making her turn king's evidence, by which her mother Anne is hanged as a witch.

1648 Siege of Colchester – a Royalist force under Lord Goring is besieged by a Parliamentarian army under Sir Thomas Fairfax. This lasts 11 weeks from 13 June to 28 August. Sir Charles Lucas and Sir George Lisle, two of the Royalist commanders, are briefly imprisoned in Colchester Castle after the siege, then executed in the bailey. A fine of £12,000 is imposed on the townspeople, half being paid by the Dutch congregation, but with £2,000 later returned for relief of the poor.

1656   James Parnell, a Quaker imprisoned for his faith after preaching at Colchester and Coggeshall, dies in 'the oven' at Colchester Castle on 4 May; he was 19 years old.

1665   Plague strikes the town killing over 4,500 people (half the population) between August 1665 and December 1666. London lost about a quarter of its citizens and sent £1,000 aid.

1669   Duke Cosmo of Florence visits Colchester and is shown the effects of the siege. In his entourage was Sir Bernard Gascoigne, once a Royalist officer, who had avoided execution.

1692   Severe earthquake affects the town; St Peter's church is greatly damaged. The medieval church had a central tower and was cruciform in shape.

1694   John Wheeley, a local ironmonger, having bought Colchester Castle in 1683, now demolishes the upper storey and corner towers with the aid of screws and gunpowder.

1698   Celia Fiennes, the celebrated diarist, on a visit to Colchester observes that 'the whole town is employed in spinning, weaving, washing, drying, and dressing their bays'.

1710   The Bluecoat School is opened in Culver Street as a Church Charity to prepare about 100 boys and girls for apprenticeship or service.

1722   Daniel Defoe leases Severalls Estate from the corporation on a 99-year lease; he was then writing the story of *Moll Flanders*, modelled on a girl from nearby Mile End.

1727   Charles Gray MP, a local lawyer, marries Sarah Creffield and is given the Castle by her mother, Mary Webster, as a wedding present.

Almshouses are founded by Arthur Winsley, an alderman and wealthy cloth-merchant, who established a charity for 12 Colchester men aged over 60 who had 'fallen into decay'.

1728   The Dutch Church and Dutch Bay Company are finally wound up, officers for the latter having been sworn in for the last time in January.

1733   The 'flying shuttle' is invented by John Kay of Bury, Lancashire, while living in Colchester.

1748   The Revd Philip Morant, celebrated Rector of St Mary's-at-the-Walls (1737-70), publishes his *History and Antiquities of Colchester*.

1758   John Wesley preaches in Colchester for the first time, a meeting-house being built in the following year near the present Castle Methodist church in Maidenburgh Street.

1764   Theatre built on part of the Moot Hall yard and leased to the Norwich Company of Comedians.

1765   The Mayor's Chain, made of 506 gold links in 6 separate loops, is presented to the mayor, baymaker Thomas Wilshire, by a grateful London cloth merchant, Leonard Ellington.

1775   John Howard, the prison reformer, makes one of 4 visits to the County Gaol in Colchester Castle in October, where typhus had just killed the head gaoler.

1783   Double oil-lamps, installed in the High Street by the Channel Commissioners with funds levied as harbour dues at the Hythe, provide Colchester's first street lighting.

1791   Almshouses are founded in Military Road by John Kendall and his wife Anne, who were Quakers. These were initially for eight poor women aged 60 and over.

1794   First infantry barracks are built, after a successful appeal to the corporation by local innkeepers complaining of the very expensive billeting on them of troops.

1795   Queen Charlotte is presented with a gift of candied eryngo or sea holly on a visit to the town, thus helping to enhance the popularity of this local delicacy.

1808   The Colchester Waterworks Company is enabled by Act of Parliament to build a pumping station and two large reservoirs at the foot of Balkerne Hill.

1811   Jane and Ann Taylor move to Ongar from West Stockwell Street, where they had composed many popular children's works including Jane's *Twinkle, Twinkle Little Star*.

1819   First or foundation stone of the Essex and Colchester Hospital laid by Lord Braybrooke, HM Lord Lieutenant of Essex, on Friday 18 June (Waterloo Day).

Gas lighting is first installed in High Street, with chemists Harris & Firmin as contractors, who had manufactured coal gas to light their own and adjacent shops there since 1817.

1821   Corn Exchange, with insurance office above (now the Essex and Suffolk Fire Office), is built on the site of the Dutch Bay Hall in High Street.

1836   A full-time police force, consisting of a superintendent and 19 men, is formed to replace the part-time parish constables.

1837   Colchester Union Workhouse (later St Mary's Hospital) is built to a design by John Brown of Norwich; it could accommodate nearly 400 sick, destitute and aged paupers.

1838   Gasworks built at The Hythe: variously improved, extended and rebuilt, they were closed in 1971 and demolished two years later on Colchester's conversion to North Sea gas.

1843   Eastern Counties Railway from London to Colchester North Station is formally opened for passengers on 29 March. Goods traffic had begun on 7 March.

First or foundation stone of the new Town Hall is laid with masonic ceremonial by Roger Nunn Esq. MD, Mayor, on 13 September, after demolition of the medieval Moot Hall.

1845   Colchester Oyster Feast, replacing the Corporation Luncheon, is first held on 20 October during the mayoralty of Alderman Henry Wolton, who invited 200 guests at his own expense.

1850   Charles Haddon Spurgeon hears a sermon, which leads to his conversion, at the Primitive Methodist Chapel in Artillery Street on the morning of Sunday 6 January.

1853   Colchester Royal Grammar School, on removal from Culver Street to new buildings by H.H. Hayward in Lexden Road, is opened at the present site on 4 August.

1855   Wooden huts, erected on the Ordnance Field as temporary infantry barracks, were the modern garrison's first buildings; they were replaced in brick in 1896–1904.

1857   Middle Row (medieval shops built by the early 14th century) is removed from the east end of St Runwald's church in High Street.

1859   Eastern Counties' Asylum is established at Essex Hall, where the Railway Hotel built in the Italianate style in 1843, was converted to a hospital for the mentally handicapped in 1850.

1860   Museum, combining the collections of the Colchester Corporation and the Essex Archaeological Society, is opened in the crypt of Colchester Castle on 27 September.

1861   Colchester Co-operative Society is founded at a general meeting held in the Public Hall on 13 May, John Castle and a Mr Dand being the initiators.

1862   Cattle market is removed from High Street to a new site outside the North Gate at Middleborough, where it remained until removal to Severalls Lane in 1974.

1865   Engineering firm of Davey, Paxman and Davey is first established at the Standard Ironworks in Culver Street, moving to Hythe Hill in 1876.

1866   Colchester becomes headquarters of the army's new Eastern District, with 11 counties under the command of its General Officer Commanding.

1870   Colne Oyster Fishery is recovered by the corporation by Act of Parliament and a joint board is established with the fishery company.

1874   New Post Office, built by George Dobson of Colchester, is opened in Head Street (on removal from High Street) on 26 June.

1878   Colchester Fire Brigade is formed as a uniformed volunteer force of 14 men under the chief constable; the Colchester Corporation Fire Brigade was created in 1896.

St Runwald's Church, built in the late 11th/early 12th century, is demolished and its site sold to the town council to widen the High Street.

1883   Balkan Water Tower, nicknamed Jumbo, is formally dedicated to public use by the Mayor, Alderman John Bawtree Harvey, on 27 September.

1884   Colchester Earthquake, with its epicentre at Peldon and *c.*5.25 on the Richter Scale, lasts for several seconds at 9.20am on 22 April; several buildings in the area are damaged.

Sewage works open on 31 July at the Hythe, on land bought by the Council from coal merchant Thomas Moy in 1880.

1892   Sir George Biddell Airy, Astronomer Royal 1836–81, who was brought up in George Street and educated at the Grammar School, dies on 2 January, aged 90.

Castle Park is opened by Sir David Evans, Lord Mayor of London, on 20 October; it cost £7,600, including a bequest of £3,000 from Mr R.D. Catchpool.

1894   First Public Library is opened in West Stockwell Street by the Rt Hon Baron Herschell, Lord High Chancellor of England, on 25 October.

1898   Foundation stone of the present Town Hall is laid by HRH the Duke of Cambridge, who afterwards attended the Oyster Feast, on 31 October.

1902   Town Hall, designed by John Belcher in the Renaissance style, is opened by the Earl of Rosebery on 15 May; it cost £55,000, of which local benefactors contributed £12,000.

1904   Electric tramways established on 28 July, to link Lexden, the Hythe, East Street and North Station with the High Street. The last tram ran from Lexden on 9 December 1929.

Hospital in Lexden Road is renamed 'Essex County Hospital' and a new children's surgical ward, built at a cost of over £3,000, is opened by HRH Princess Louise.

1909   Colchester Historical Pageant, with a cast of nearly 3,000 performers directed by the playwright Louis Napoleon Parker, is held in Castle Park on 21–26 June.

1923   Unveiling and dedication of the War Memorial and a new entrance to the Castle and Castle Park, by Viscount and Viscountess Cowdray on 24 May (Empire Day).

1929   Holly Trees is opened as a 'Museum of post-Conquest Antiquities' by Annie, Viscountess Cowdray, the High Steward of Colchester, on 26 September.

1930   Camulodunum excavations, which continued annually until 1939, start at Sheepen in June; these excavations brought international renown to Colchester and its archaeology.

1933   New By-Pass Road opened by the Rt Hon Viscount Ullswater on 29 June. Built over 3½ miles at a cost of £292,000, it employed a weekly average of 300 local men.

1935   Colchester Castle, re-roofed with extended museum accommodation, is opened by Sir Charles Peers, Chief Inspector of Ancient Monuments, on 12 July.

1937   Colchester Repertory Theatre opens in the Albert Hall on Saturday 2 October, remaining there until its last performance on Saturday 22 January 1972.

1944   St Botolph's Corner is set alight when about 1,400 incendiaries and 8 phosphorous oil bombs are dropped on the town around midnight on 25 February.

1948   Colchester Mercury, the finest Roman bronze statuette in Britain, is acquired by Colchester Museum, having been ploughed up about three years earlier at Gosbecks Farm.

1955   St Nicholas's church, rebuilt by world famous Victorian architect Sir George Gilbert Scott in 1875–6, is demolished; on its site in High Street now stands St Nicholas House.

1958   Natural History Museum is opened in the former All Saints church by Sir George Dyson on 24 September.

1964   University of Essex admits its first students (about 120) on a 200-acre site at Wivenhoe Park given by Essex County Council, a royal charter being granted in 1965.

1971   Colchester United beat Leeds United 3-2 in the 5th round of the FA Cup, before a crowd of 16,000 at Layer Road on 13 February.

1972   Mercury Theatre, designed by Norman Downie and built with seating for 500 at a cost of £260,000, is opened by the Rt Hon Jenny Lee MP on 10 May.

1974   Holy Trinity church, after several years of dereliction, opens as a Museum of Social History; it was purchased by the council for a nominal £200 donated by the Soroptimists.

1980   Central Library, built as part of the Lion Walk development to replace the premises in Shewell Road, is opened in Trinity Square on 9 May.

1985   Colchester District General Hospital is officially opened by HM Queen Elizabeth II, after whom it is named, on 17 May.

Colchester and NE Essex branch of the Essex Record Office officially opened in Stanwell Street by Dr Geoffrey Martin, Keeper of the Public Records, on 7 June.

1986   St Helena Hospice formally opened at Myland Hall by Queen Elizabeth the Queen Mother on Friday 11 April.

1987   Tymperleys Museum is opened by the Mayor, Councillor Bob Russell, to display over 200 Colchester clocks bequeathed to the Borough by Bernard Mason, on Saturday 16 May.

1989   Chapel of Colchester Castle, its new roof funded by Kent Blaxill Ltd and a government grant, is opened by Arts Minister, Rt Hon Richard Luce MP, on Wednesday 22 March.

Divisional Police Headquarters are opened in Butt Road by the Rt Hon Douglas Hurd MP, Home Secretary, on Thursday 21 September.

1991   High Woods Country Park and Visitor Centre are officially opened by Chris Packham, naturalist and TV presenter, on Saturday 1 June.

1992   Completion of the council's 8-phase programme of repairs to the external fabric of Colchester Castle which was begun in 1983 at an estimated cost of £500,000.

1995   Gosbecks Archaeological Park launched by the Mayor, Councillor Mrs. Mary Fairhead, who accepts 162 acres (65.5 ha) of farmland from the Barbour family on Monday 7 August.

These entries have been extracted from a longer version of dated events by Mark Davies, entitled *Colchester's Chronology*, which is being published separately.

Chapter 1
Around the Town

We begin our pictorial exploration of the Changing Face of Colchester by discovering to what extent the town itself has changed and developed over the last 200 or so years. Various types of illustrative material has been used ranging from 18th century watercolours, right through to the latest digitally produced photographs, all of which combine to reveal a vivid and extraordinary glimpse of Colchester's more recent past. As mentioned above, the earliest images included in the section are from the 18th century, which of course enables us take a brief look back at life as it was lived in an age which was totally removed from any of the trappings of modern life. No made up streets or footpaths, no public transport, fewer people and a distinct rural feeling about the place. The majority of illustrations featured, however, date from the 1850s which of course was also the age of photography, an invention that was to leave an indelible mark on our recent past.

Most of the early photographs produced in the years leading up to World War One were topographical in nature, capturing street scenes and important buildings, and were largely published in the form of picture postcards, the collection of which became something of a national pastime during the late Victorian and Edwardian years. As time went on the photographers ventured more into the interior of buildings capturing images of school classrooms, shop interiors and people working in local factories, all of which combine to portray a fuller picture of life in the past.

And it is part of this unique documentary record that is presented in this publication, both as a series of individual images, which may each be enjoyed within their own historical context but also, where possible, the images selected have been included as part of a small compilation of images covering the same subject, over an extended period. So for instance, in many cases, it will be possible to view an area or section of the town as it would have appeared to at least three generations of Colcestrians, each with its own particular atmosphere and charm. In the main, most images of the town produced before World War One are likely to feature such things as horse-drawn carriages and trams, and ladies walking the pavements in their long skirts, literally sweeping the streets as they walked.

By the 1920s you will see that most of the horses have disappeared, having been replaced with motor vehicles, and by the 1930s the trams had also given way to motor buses. In later years the streets will be seen full of motor vehicles as we move nearer to our own times. The buildings have also changed – from small family run businesses and shops at the turn of the last century, to the large plate glass windowed buildings of the modern department stores.

An early view of Culver Street dating from 1857. The picture was taken from a point near the junction with Queen Street and is seen looking west with the wall of All Saints' Church on the right. Culver Street was formerly known as Back Lane and most of the buildings on the right of the street originally extended through to the High Street which ran in a parallel direction. Note the central drainage gutter running along the middle of the street.

This view of Culver Street was taken from a similar position sometime in the 1930s. It provides us with a nice close up of the buildings on the left which were demolished in 1939 to make room for a car park. The buildings were mainly of timber-frame construction and part of one the buildings, seen just beyond the lamp standard on the left, was saved from destruction and re-erected in the Castle Museum.

Culver Street once again, but this time looking in an easterly direction towards Queen Street. The building on the right housing Adam's & Co Motor Engineers was the former site of the Colchester Grammar School before its removal to Lexden Road in 1853. The garage business itself had evolved out of an earlier horse-drawn carriage building firm which had moved into the old school premises.

Two contrasting views showing the entrance to Culver Street from the Head Street end. The earlier view at the top was taken in the 1940s before the café on the right corner was demolished and the entrance widened. The shop on the left was Forsdike & Bonner, a well-known family grocers whose presence was usually indicated by the wafting aroma of freshly roasting coffee. The lower picture shows the current view with the Halifax Building Society premises dominating the entire right-hand corner.

An early view of the High Street looking west from a position close to the War Memorial and entrance to the Castle Park. The picture was certainly taken before the rebuilding of St Nicholas's Church in 1874 and shows the ruins of the old church with its 18th-century timber-boarded tower and projecting 'frying pan' clock. Note the partly cobbled and rather uneven road surface which was a feature of most highways at this time being some years before the advent of tarmacadam. The pavements, however, appear to be reasonably well paved.

In this similar view of the High Street taken some 60 or 70 years later, the high gothic spire of the new St Nicholas's Church dominates the scene. On the left is John Bedwell's jewellery, pawnbroking and clothing business and adjoining is the retail outlet of Adams' Garages Ltd. The next building along the row, with the arched windows, is the Sea Horse Inn, one of the town's many rendezvous points for the carrier trade providing stabling for the horses. Parking a car at this time of day obviously presented few problems.

A close up view of the Sea Horse Inn taken at the time of Queen Victoria's Golden Jubilee in 1887. To the left of the inn John Bedwell is at this time trading as an upholsterer and furniture dealer, and like most of the town centre traders of the day was pleased to display his patriotism and support of the Queen's Golden Jubilee year with a lavishly decorated shop front.

By the 1970s the High Street had taken on a much more modern appearance. St Nicholas's Church has been replaced with a department store, modern 1960s style buildings have appeared on the right of the street and the days of horse-drawn carriages and casual parking for cars in the High Street have long gone.

This charming watercolour painting of the High Street, seen looking west in the 1890s, is the work of Major John Edward Bale, formerly of the West Indian Regiment and a veteran of the Ashanti War in 1873. After retiring from the army, and settling in Colchester, Major Bale became a prolific artist sketching and painting many features of the town's landscape up to his death in 1913. In this composition, one can note the Red Lion Hotel on the left of the street, and on the right is the old Victorian Town Hall with flag flying. A particular feature of many of the major's paintings is the inclusion of a military figure or two. In this case, note the soldier standing on the left hand pavement saluting an officer passing by on horseback.

Within a few years of Major Bale's painting of the High Street, the scene was to undergo a dramatic change with the building of the new Town Hall. The new building added a touch of grandeur to the town's principle street and was officially opened on 15 May 1902. This particular view dates from 1903 and shows a horse-drawn omnibus outside the Red Lion Hotel on the left, an approaching steam lorry in the distance and a group of horse cabbies waiting at the cab rank in front of the Town Hall.

A relatively modern view of the High Street from the 1970s showing the Town Hall still impressively dominating the scene. The large Victorian water tower (Jumbo) still looms in the background, but apart from that the street reflects much more of the modern age, particularly as far as the mode of transport is concerned. To the Edwardian public, however, such a futuristic scene would have been hard for them to imagine, and likewise we too would probably be somewhat surprised were we able to view the same scene a hundred or so years into the future.

A comparatively rare view of the High Street looking west around 1860. The rarity comes in the fact that Jumbo, the famous water tower, which currently stands overlooking the western end of the High Street had yet to be built. Before the building of the new Town Hall in 1902, it would appear that most commercial photographers preferred to capture the view looking towards the east with its wide street and the gothic spire of St Nicholas's Church. St Runwald's Church seen here standing in the middle of the street was demolished in 1878.

The High Street looking east in the late 1890s and the preferred viewpoint of most commercial photographers before the building of the new Town Hall in 1902. The hansom cab is standing on the former site of St Runwald's Church, which since its demolition in 1878 added greatly to the width of this section of the High Street.

This view of the High Street looking east and showing the old Town Hall and St Runwald's Church has to date from before 1862 when the cattle market was moved from the High Street to the foot of North Hill. In this view one can see the cattle and sheep pens in place along the south side of the street, although whether the picture was taken before or after the sale is not clear. The picture was, of course, taken before the development of snapshot photography as clearly evidenced by the blurred images of the two men in the foreground.

An interesting view of the lower High Street taken in 1887 as preparations are under way to celebrate the Queen's Golden Jubilee. This was one of several archways erected spanning the main streets which were then decorated with evergreens and flowers. The buildings to the left of the arch, which included L.J. Watts, monumental mason, and H.W. Goody's newsagents and printing works were later pulled down to make way for the new entrance to the castle park. Through the arch can be seen the holly trees standing outside what is now Holly Trees Museum, and beyond the trees can be seen Frere House which was demolished in the 1930s and the space turned into garden.

The same section of High Street seen from the opposite direction. The bay windowed building on the left is the present Visitor Information Centre and at the end of the row of buildings on the right is the Castle Inn, another survivor to the present day.

A modern day view of East Hill looking towards the town centre. Most of the buildings seen in the picture are survivors from a bygone age ranging from numerous timber-frame structures to Georgian buildings. Part of St James the Great Church can be seen rising above the buildings on the left from its position just inside the old Roman wall. In fact, the bus seen ascending the hill is passing over the very spot where once stood the Roman East Gate.

A decorated archway erected at the bottom of East Hill as part of the Queen's Golden Jubilee celebrations. After weeks of preparations the event finally took place on 21 June 1887 with most of the town having taken on something of a carnival appearance. The people of Colchester turned out in their thousands to join in the fun which included a mass procession through the main streets, followed by a grand fête on the Abbey Fields.

This Colchester street would be almost unrecognisable today were it not for the tall building seen at the end of the street on the left, and the small gable-fronted building in the background. The latter building is, of course, now known as 'Cheap Jacks' and we are looking east along Culver Street in 1940. The building in the left corner was the rear entrance to Woolworths, and which is now the location of Dixon's electrical store. The buildings on the right have since made way for a number of new precinct shops including the British Home Stores.

The Colchester and East Essex Co-operative Society have traded from this prime position on the corner of Culver Street and Long Wyre Street since Victorian times. The picture was taken in 1940 in the early years of World War Two and despite the constant threat of German air raids occurring, life still had to lived and shopping had to be done.

A modern day view of Culver Street looking east from a similar position to that shown opposite.

This view of Balkerne Hill was captured just a few years before the road was swallowed up during the construction of a new dual carriageway in the mid-1970s. The remains of the Roman wall can be seen on the left of the road and at the top of the hill, sitting astride the old Roman gateway, is the King's Head (now the Hole in the Wall) public house. The pub and remains of the gateway of course still survive, but the houses on the right have vanished.

An old drawing of Balkerne Hill showing the Roman wall on the left, and the King's Head public house on the brow of the hill.

The Balkerne Hill dual carriageway as it appears today.

Two contrasting views showing the lower section of Balkerne Hill looking in the direction of North Hill. The top picture again captures the scene shortly before the redevelopment of the area in the 1970s. The railings of the former cattle market site can just be seen on the left, and the white plastered buildings seen on the right follow the line of the Roman wall. As can be seen in the modern viewpoint below the scene would be barely recognisable were it not for the small gable-fronted building seen at the bottom of North Hill in the background.

A late 15th-century timber-framed building seen both before and after restoration. The building is located in West Stockwell Street just opposite the junction with St Runwald's Street. As can be seen, the building had been much altered over the centuries before being heavily restored after World War One. In some respects the restoration may have been a little too heavy – the wall studs, for instance, have been fastened with nails!

This rather charming view of West Stockwell Street is seen looking up in the direction of the High Street. The picture dates from the early 1900s and presents the street in a picturesque form with its profusion of timber-framed buildings. It was probably for this very reason that the internationally renowned architect, Nikolaus Pevsner, also referred to the street as 'perhaps the most attractive street of Colchester'.

This 18th-century view of Mersea Road observed from a point near to the present St Botolph's roundabout would be totally unrecognisable today were it not for the tell-tale buttresses seen supporting the wall of the former St John's Abbey gardens a short distance beyond the row of buildings on the right. The building on the near right with the pargetting on the plasterwork was the old Woolpack Inn, while at the top of the hill can be seen the old Mersea Road windmill which survived until 1813 when it was replaced with a brick tower mill.

The present day view of Mersea Road showing the abbey wall and supporting buttresses.

Two further pictures of Mersea Road dating from around 1909. In the top picture we are looking up Mersea Road from the junction with Magdalen Street known as Plough Corner. The bottom picture was taken from a position midway up Mersea Road hill looking down in the direction of Plough Corner. In 1911, Colchester's first purpose made cinema – the Vaudeville – was erected near the buildings seen on the right beyond the group of children.

This view of St Botolph's Street dating from the early 1890s was taken from the junction with Queen Street looking towards Mersea Road. Motorised transport of any form had yet to arrive in the town and the street appears to have been a pedestrian's paradise. Note the two gentlemen standing having a conversation in the middle of the road.

About 40 years separates these two views of St Botolph's Street looking north in the direction of Queen Street. The top picture was taken in the 1890s and despite the distinct lack of any traffic, horse-drawn or otherwise, the shoppers appear to be keeping fairly well to the footpaths. By the time that the lower picture had been taken in the 1930s, the town's electric tramway system had come and gone and, in this view, the solitary motor car seen travelling up what is now a one way street, appears to be outnumbered by cyclists.

This view shows the lower part of North Hill looking towards Middleborough in 1858. The building seen in the centre of the picture projecting towards the centre of the road was all that remained of the old medieval North Gate. The gateway itself formed an integral part of a three storey timber-framed building which spanned the entire roadway, the upper floors being used for accommodation purposes. The central gateway and corresponding upper floors were removed in 1774 following a partial collapse, and much of the remainder was cleared in 1823.

This watercolour painting dating from around 1775 is believed to show the remaining section of the North Gate following its partial removal in 1774. The painting does, however, appear to show one or two inconsistencies with other known images of the gateway, particularly with design of the roof and the position of the gateway. The artist concerned is believed to have been Edward Eyre who is known to have painted others scenes in the town.

This representation of the North Gate as depicted on Pryor's Prospect of Colchester in 1724, is the only known image of the gate in its complete form. Notice the ridge of the main roof spanning the road with its three projecting gables, and the centrally placed gateway. Now compare these features with the images of the gate on the opposite page.

Another view showing the lower part of North Hill taken in 1940. The entrance to the cattle market can be seen on the left, and the road runs in a nice unbroken line as far as the eye can see – much unlike the present day configuration of roundabouts, bus lanes and one way system.

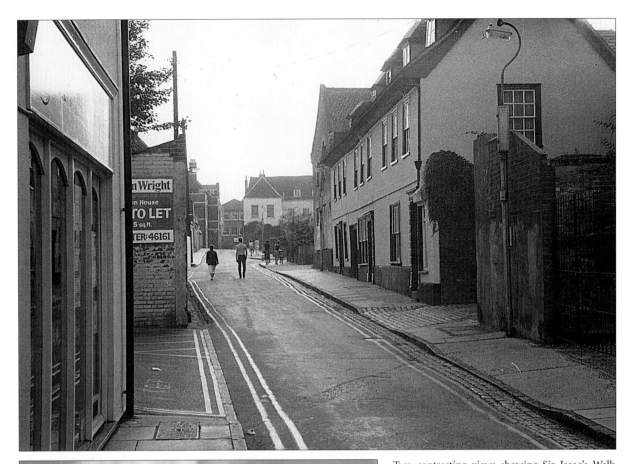

Two contrasting views showing Sir Isaac's Walk which runs along the inside of the town wall. The upper picture was taken in 1983 shortly before work began on redeveloping this part of town. The only building of note in an otherwise motley assortment of dilapidated buildings, is the fine early 18th-century building seen here on the right. By the time that the bottom picture (from the reverse angle) had been taken, however, the street had been transformed into a rather splendid row of traditionally built retail outlets. If nothing else, a street has been created which is entirely suitable for the 18th-century building to stand in. This has to be one occasion when the town planners and developers have got it right.

An interesting view of the western end of Sir Isaac's Walk looking towards Head Street. The picture must have been taken before 1909 because this was when the present large brick building which stands on the left-hand corner was built.

Here we have two views of St John's Street taken from Headgate Corner both before and after the building of the Playhouse theatre which opened in March 1929. For the first 18 months after opening there was a weekly change of live shows in the 1,150 seater building before the owners began to realise that the showing of films would be more profitable. In September 1930, therefore, a screen was installed and the Playhouse became the town's fourth house to show films.

Two further contrasting views of St John's Street looking east and taken about 70 years apart. The top picture dates from the early 1900s and shows the type of horse-drawn traffic that was the norm of the day. The street was also an alternative route for those wishing to avoid the High Street as they passed through the town. The bottom picture was taken in 1975 and shows the car park and other buildings on the right which were demolished to make way for the present shopping centre.

A fairly quiet looking Crouch Street seen from Headgate Corner in the 1890s. However, don't be fooled by the presence of hardly any traffic, because even before the days of motorised transport, this particular stretch of road was the A12 of the times catering for every type of traffic passing between London and the coast. Note the point duty policeman standing discreetly on the left pavement.

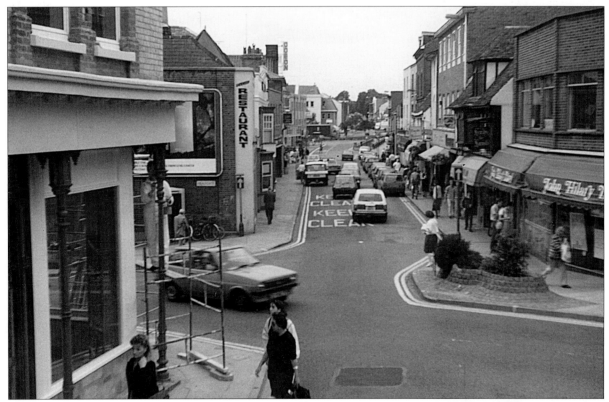

By the 1980s, when this picture was taken, Crouch Street had been relegated to little more than a service road providing access to a dozen or so shops.

Crouch Street looking towards Headgate Corner in 1926. Note the approaching tram en route to Lexden and the open top car outside the Bull Commercial Hotel. In the days of the horse-drawn carrier trade, the Bull was a popular rendezvous point for carriers travelling to and from various villages to the south and west of town, providing stabling facilities for the horses.

Headgate Corner in 1934. The policeman on point duty has to keep his wits about him as traffic approaches from four different directions. At this time of day the constable would share the point duty work with a colleague, each spending an hour at a time directing traffic, whilst the other patrolled the streets. In cold weather they were allowed a mat to stand on to prevent their feet from freezing to the ground.

A charming view of St Mary's steps from the early 1900s. The opening in the Roman wall originated from a small arched drain which was subsequently enlarged to provide a convenient access point through the wall. The children are probably pupils of St Mary's School which is just out of picture to the left. At break times, the children used to exercise in a section of the nearby churchyard.

The former St Mary's school building erected in front of the Roman wall in 1864. The school could accommodate about 130 children in its two adjoining classrooms, but inevitably was to always experience problems with overcrowding. The building was demolished in the 1970s to make way for the new dual-carriageway.

The present day view of the St Mary's Church and Roman wall. Despite the introduction of a new road system, the steps provide a convenient access to and from the town centre.

St Mary's Church and nearby buildings as depicted in 1824. Note the ramshackle building leaning against the Roman wall, a typical feature of earlier times, and the repair to the top of the church tower resulting from damage sustained during the Siege of Colchester in 1648.

Two views showing the public house which sits astride the Roman gateway at the top of Balkerne Hill. The top view dates from 1932 and shows the pub as it was then known as the King's Head, a name deriving from the time of the Siege of Colchester, and the subsequent trial and beheading of King Charles I in 1649. Today the pub is known as The Hole in the Wall, a reminder of when a former publican decided to remove a section of the ancient monument in order to provide his regulars with a better view of the newly constructed railway on the outskirts of town.

St Nicholas's Passage looking north towards the High Street in 1940. The little girl seen walking alongside her mother is probably of a similar age now to the elderly lady seen walking a few paces ahead of her in this picture. Note also the presence of St Nicholas's Church which was later demolished in the 1950s.

This present day view of St Nicholas's Passage depicts a far busier thoroughfare complete with modern shop fronts. The church, of course, has gone although part of the graveyard still survives behind a modern brick wall.

An early view of the High Street looking east from the top of North Hill in 1831. The colonnaded building in the foreground, known locally as the Fire Office, was erected in 1819 to serve as both an insurance office and corn exchange. The Doric fluted columns are of cast iron as is most of the external cladding of the building. The last thing that a fire insurance company would have wanted was for their building to be destroyed by fire! This section of High Street was also the location of the weekly cattle market before its removal to Middleborough in 1862.

A similar view of the High Street dating from about 1903. By this time the Corn Exchange had moved to a new location further down the street, and the space in front of the Fire Office was being used as a horse cab rank. The two cabs depicted, a hansom and a landau, were among more than a hundred similar vehicles plying the streets of Colchester in the years before World War One.

By the 1950s horse transport on the streets of Colchester had become a thing of the past, although the Fire Office remained as a regular stopping place for public transport. This was also to be the last full decade that was to see a two-way traffic system still operating in the High Street, an almost inconceivable situation by modern day standards. Note also the second floor extension to the Fire Office.

A modern view of the above scene showing the one-way traffic system in operation. The pavements have also been made a lot wider, leaving just a single lane for traffic.

A rare photograph showing the old Post Office building in Head Street at the time of Queen Victoria's Golden Jubilee. To the right of the Post Office can be seen The Alexandra public house which closed down in 1913, and which later reopened as a Navy and Army surplus store at the end of World War One. The business later developed into a general clothing store which continued trading until its closure in 2001. Finally, note the clock in the niche on the Post Office wall which was always set to display London time (GMT) as opposed to Local time which was a few minutes behind.

This view of Shewell Road, taken from Sir Isaac's Walk and looking towards Culver Street, in 1940 no longer exists having been swallowed up in the development of the Culver Shopping Precinct in the 1980s. The only feature which has, in part, survived to claim a place in the new precinct, is the old library building seen here at the end of the street on the right.

A view showing part of the Culver Shopping Precinct which opened in 1987. Part of the old library building, with its small multi-glazed windows, can just be seen in the background. The precinct itself overlies a central part of the former Roman legionary fortress which was erected on the western side of the present town in AD 43. Prior to work commencing on the new development, an extensive archaeological excavation took place which revealed evidence of several streets and over 20 buildings belonging to the fortress, including the remains of a granary and six barrack blocks used to house the soldiers.

Lion Walk is another of the town centre streets which has vanished from the scene, once again to make way for a new shopping development. Formerly known as Cat Lane, the street is located at the eastern extremity of the original Roman fortress and, as would be expected, numerous Roman finds were encountered during excavation work prior to building work commencing. The Gothic style church was built in 1863 on the site of an earlier foundation and although the building has since been extensively remodelled (only the original tower remains), it claims to be the oldest non-conformist church in Colchester being able to trace its original congregation back to at least 1642.

Lion Walk as it appears today. The church tower is all that remains from the earlier picture.

This picture portrays the current view from the top end of Lion Walk as seen on the older photograph (opposite) at the far end of street.

Here we have two views looking down Maidenburgh Street taken over a hundred years apart. The earlier picture at the top dates from 1898 and the one below from December 2002. Despite some alterations to the road layout and the replacement and remodelling of a few buildings, the street would still be instantly recognisable to those residents in the earlier scene.

This section of Priory Street looking towards East Hill from a point near what is now The Dell was taken in 1933 some few years before the row of houses on the left were demolished to make way for a car park. The street was formerly known as More Lane, so named from the nearby more or garden which belonged to St Botolph's Priory.

The view of Priory Street, from the same angle, as it appears today.

This charming watercolour painting dating from the 1770s shows the old river crossing at East Bridge. The view is seen looking away from the town towards East Street and the Old Siege House which can be seen behind the small group of trees. The bridge at this time was for pedestrian use only with carts and wagons having to ford the river. The field on the left with cattle grazing still survives as a small recreation ground, and the small gabled building seen on the near right side of the footbridge may also still survive in the form of a rather dilapidated barn. Note also the windmill in the background which stood up near the Harwich Road.

This modern day view of the above scene illustrates the extent to which the landscape has changed over the last 200 or so years. Whilst the general street plan and one or two buildings may still remain, the overall rustic, or pastoral, feel of the place has been lost to time.

This view from 1867 shows a number of sailing barges moored alongside East Mill shortly after the channel between here and The Hythe had been widened sufficiently to allow the barges access. Even so, the short journey from The Hythe was not without difficulties as the barges had to be manoeuvered below four low bridges in what was a fairly shallow draught of water. This usually meant lowering the mast and rigging at the Hythe and literally pushing the barge up river by means of long poles or booms, one end of which was placed against your shoulder and the other in the river or on the bank as you walked the length of the barge pushing your way along.

The old mill buildings as they appear today after being converted into a hotel in 1979. The last of the old Thames sailing craft to venture this far upriver was a barge called *The Raven* which it was hoped could be converted into some kind of floating restaurant. Unfortunately, despite the efforts of two former barge hands, Frank Thompson and Jim Lawrenson, who negotiated the barge upriver beneath four low bridges in the mid-1980s, the barge was never converted and was allowed to deteriorate beyond repair.

This charming view of East Bridge looking in the direction of the town centre was painted by Major John Bale in the 1890s. The bridge depicted, consisting of five brick arches, was built in 1802 from finance provided by a turnpike at Lexden. The bridge was rebuilt in its present form in 1928 as part of a road widening scheme.

East bridge as it appears today from a similar viewpoint. The former hump in the middle of the crossing has been removed, and the road considerably widened, but this is really as far as the improvements have gone resulting in a much more bland and less interesting structure.

Almost every foot of mooring space in this view of the Hythe from the early 1900s appears to have been taken up by a flotilla of Thames sailing barges. There was stiff competition among the barge owners and skippers as they competed for the rich pickings of the river trade that was available at the time. Sadly this ancient port has recently closed bringing to an end a centre of local activity stretching back over 800 years.

Here we have two views of East Mill and the adjacent road bridge spanning a period of nearly 150 years. The top view dates from 1858 and shows the mill before it was extensively remodelled in the 1880s. The lower view was taken in 2001 and shows the remodelled version of the mill which is now been used as a hotel. Note also the much flattened 1928 road bridge.

An almost unrecognisable view of the Rose and Crown hotel as seen in 1897. The front of the building is fully plastered hiding the extensive timber-framing which is now such a prominent feature of the hotel. The present Old Coach Road seen running to the right of the building was in former times the main Ipswich Road leading from Colchester into Suffolk.

The Rose and Crown hotel as seen today.

This interesting view of the lower section of Harwich Road as seen looking towards St Andrew's Avenue dates from the early 1930s. A horse-drawn delivery van can be seen on the left of the picture outside the local Co-operative store, next to which is the Clarendon Inn. Note also the early motor cars depicted and the approaching single decker bus which is on route to the Drury Hotel.

As can be seen from this modern viewpoint of Harwich Road, very little has changed in the intervening 70 or so years. One noticeable addition however, is the row of bells seen suspended high across the road. These were put in place in the 1960s when the rail track was electrified as a warning to high vehicles approaching the crossing.

These two views of the old bypass looking west from the Harwich Road roundabout show that relatively little has changed over the 70 or so years which separate the pictures. The top picture was taken during the construction of the road in the early 1930s and shows a gang of men working on the new roundabout. The new road took over three years to complete with most of the work being completed by the locally unemployed who were obliged to do their turn on the road in order to qualify for their dole money.

Two contrasting views of Ipswich Road seen looking north from a position near the junction with Goring Road. The top picture dates from the early 1930s and shows an early corporation bus returning to town from the terminus at St John's church. The bus was one of a new fleet of vehicles which had superseded the town's old trams in 1929. The lower view was taken from a similar viewpoint in 2002 and illustrates the changes seen over the last 70 or so years.

A policeman is seen taking details at the scene of this traffic accident in Barrack Street in 1933. The picture was taken looking towards the Hythe from the junction with Brook Street and Wimpole Road and despite the relatively quite appearance of the street, the accident has probably arisen as both vehicles were negotiating this rather awkward junction. The row of small cottages seen on the right of the picture are believed to have been used by officers serving in the old Napoleonic barracks which occupied land to the right of Barrack Street.

Apart from the demise of the row of cottages on the right of the street, most of the buildings seen in this view of Barrack Street, taken in 2002, remain much the same as they did 70 years earlier.

In this view of the same junction we are looking south towards Wimpole Road from the top of Brook Street. The street appears quite deserted although the tyre marks seen in the foreground would indicate quite recent activity. The tram lines seen crossing the junction would date the picture to before 1929.

Once again we can compare the earlier scene with how the junction appears today. The most striking difference can be seen in the increased width of the entrance into Wimpole Road, straight ahead.

This rather charming view of Winsley's almshouses in Old Heath Road was drawn in 1801 and shows the original range of accommodation erected in accordance with the will of Arthur Winsley in 1726. His will had directed that accommodation be provided for, 'Twelve Ancient Men, that have lived well, and fallen into decay…'. Each man was to be above the age of 60 years and not to be considered profane, or given to swearing, drinking or any other vice.

In this modern view of Winsley's almshouses, one can see how the site has developed over the years, and at the time of writing the complex extends to 85 houses of varying designs.

This photograph from the 1870s showing the Bergholt and Nayland roads converging at North Station would appear to have taken from a fairly high vantage point, possibly from the upper floor or roof of the former Eastern Counties Asylum. The building standing where the two roads converge was the Railway Tavern, and latterly the Colchester Arms. Note also the steam train standing alongside the platform.

In this modern view from a similar vantage point, one can see that a new roundabout has all but swallowed up the entire area. The entrance to Bergholt Road can be seen on the far aside of the roundabout and the houses depicted are probably some of those shown on the earlier picture.

Very little change appears to have taken place in these two views of Maldon Road taken nearly a century apart. The pictures were taken looking towards the town centre from a position near the junction with Errington Road. Note the complete lack of overhead cabling or television aerials in the older picture as well as the rough road surface complete with horse droppings.

On the other hand, these two views showing the road junction near the Leather Bottle public house in Shrub End Road testify to quite different time periods. The top picture, which dates from the early 1900s, depicts a very rural scene devoid of any road traffic and made up pavements, and has a distinct country feel about it. Whereas the lower modern view of the same road junction shows various improvements which have taken place over the years, mainly as a result of the increasing road traffic.

Here we have two quite different, yet easily recognisable views of Mile End Road looking towards the town centre. The top picture dates from the early 1900s and shows what appears to be a group of schoolboys playing in the road, apparently quite unconcerned to the danger of any approaching traffic, and an elderly gentleman seemingly rooted to the spot in the middle of the road. In the modern day view seen below it is obvious that the highway is no longer a safe place for loitering.

Chapter 2
Schooldays

In the 18th and early 19th centuries facilities for education in Colchester were extremely limited. The few schools that did exist were mainly directed toward the wealthier classes and, apart from a few Sunday Schools, only the Bluecoat School in Culver Street and the Greencoat School in Priory Street provided any regular tuition for the children of the working classes.

The situation was improved somewhat by the founding of the Anglican National School Society in 1811, and its Nonconformist counterpart the British and Foreign School Society in 1812. Both societies adopted the monitorial system of teaching whereby large numbers of children would be taught in the same classroom under the overall control of a school master or mistress, but aided in their task by a number of monitors, who were recruited from among the more able pupils in the class. After being instructed directly by the school master or mistress, the monitors would, in turn, instruct other groups of children numbering up to 20 in size. In theory, under the rules of such a system, one master could be responsible for teaching several hundred children.

By the 1860s there was a school of sorts in most parishes of the town, although conditions were generally quite cramped with as many as 90 children being crammed into some classrooms. The situation was improved somewhat in 1870 by means of W.E. Forster's Education Act which allowed for the formation of School Boards, funded by the local rates. In Colchester however, despite a deficiency of some 1,000 places, the Act was not adopted initially as the churchmen rallied together to improve matters, embarking upon a period of new construction and upgrading of existing buildings. Their efforts, although only partly successful, were sufficient to avoid the imposition of a School Board for over 20 years as they struggled to remain in control of the local educational process.

By the early 1890s, however, it had become apparent that the ever increasing financial burden of maintaining adequate school accommodation in the town was proving too much for the church authorities, and in 1892 a School Board was finally elected to oversee the matter. The new board wasted little time in putting together a programme of expansion and improvement to existing buildings, and by the turn of the century five new schools had been built to accommodate an additional 3,000 pupils. By 1908, three further schools had been built under the auspices of the new Colchester Education Committee, formed in 1903, bringing the total number of buildings under their control to 20 and providing accommodation for over 6,000 children.

The basic curriculum taught in most schools at the time revolved very much around the three Rs, although numerous other subjects were taught including history, geography, science and art. On the practical side, in order to prepare the youngsters with skills that might be of advantage to them in later life, the girls were taught cookery, needlework and laundry, while the boys were given a grounding in woodwork and gardening. At some schools the boys were also allowed to keep a few chickens or pigeons to give them experience in animal husbandry. Physical education was provided by team games such as football, cricket, netball and hockey.

During the late Victorian and Edwardian periods, popular playground activities included games such as hopscotch, hoop bowling, tops, skipping, conkers and marbles. The material for the latter activity often originating as stoppers in various mineral bottles. Occasionally the antics of the children would cause their teachers some concern, as was the case with the so-called key, nail and match game.

This somewhat dangerous pastime involved the use of an old fashioned key with a hollowed out section which would be filled with the scrapings of several red match heads, before being plugged with a stout nail. A length of string would then be attached to both the key and nail and the resultant sling directed towards a hard surface, causing the mixture within to explode. The obvious dangers inherent in such a pastime caused many schools in the town to forbid the carrying of keys during school hours.

Regarding discipline, teachers were generally far more strict than their modern counterparts. Punishment was usually designed to administer a short sharp shock, usually in the form of the cane for boys and a smack for the girls. Generally speaking, most children of the period showed a healthy respect both for authority and their elders. On one occasion, however, this authority was severely put to the test when a group of schoolboys from Barrack Street School went on strike. Some 50 boys gathered outside the main gates of the school and, armed with sticks and cudgels, endeavoured to persuade others to join them. They then commenced to march up and down the street wearing breast-cards inscribed with the words, 'Britons never shall be slaves', and 'Fall in and follow me'. Their main demands were for more holidays and less cane and their activities attracted considerable attention in both the local and national press. Upon their subsequent return to school however they soon realised that the latter of their two demands had not been granted!

This classroom scene from East Ward School in 1908 is typical of the period. The children are seated on a series of regimentally placed tiered desks all facing towards the front of the class, and appear to be working with balls of modelling clay. The girls are wearing standard pinafores while the boys are mostly clad in either Norfolk jackets with starched collars, or sailor suits. Note also the formal dress of the teacher standing to the left and the headmaster.

In this scene from the same school and date, we observe a class of boys engaged in what would appear to be an art lesson, with the subject of their endeavours being a flower held upright in a cotton reel. Note the attendance or good conduct medals worn by several of the boys.

Boys taking part in a gymnastics class at East Ward School in 1947.

By the late 1940s the art classroom at East Ward School had taken on a much more modern appearance. The room is well decorated with examples of the children's work, and their clothing is less austere and formal. The desks, however, are still set out in straight lines and facing towards the front of the class.

This picture shows a group of girls from East Ward School in 1908 practicing their stick dance routine. Their appearance would seem to suggest that they were practicing with a particular event in mind, such as a school drama or concert, or even the forthcoming Colchester Pageant.

In this rather formal, posed photograph from North Street School in the 1930s, the pupils appear to be staging some kind of exhibition of their handicraft achievements. Note the boy on the left who appears to be wearing a set of earphones from either a radio or crystal set.

A modern class in progress at North Street Primary School. The children are grouped about four to a desk in line with modern teaching methods as their teacher, Gina James, moves about the class checking on progress.

The passing of a hundred years is clearly evident in these scenes from Old Heath School in 1898 and 2002. The move from writing slates to computers is perhaps the most significant change noted, but see also the rather innovative use of space in the technology area, and the informal seating arrangements of the modern classroom.

Old Heath School – class of *c.*1900.

Old Heath School –
class of 1950.

Old Heath School – class of 2001.

These two views show that relatively little has changed in the layout of the domestic science classroom at St Helena School over the last 64 years. The top picture, which dates from 1938, shows a number of pupils mixing ingredients at their benches or by the ovens to the right. In the lower picture however, which was taken in 2002, the room has largely taken on the appearance of a formal classroom leaving just a small section near the window for doing the practical work.

Both boy and girl pupils can be seen working in the kitchen area of the modern domestic science room at St Helena School in 2002.

This picture shows a woodworking class under way at St Helena School in 1938. Each boy can be seen standing alongside his own bench, beneath which are located his tools and other equipment.

In this view of the same classroom in 2002, the subject being taught is science and the woodworking benches have given way to a series of longer benches which are each fitted with supplies of water and gas for conducting scientific experiments. In this scene, all eyes are on the teacher as she explains details of an experiment from the blackboard.

Class teacher, Faith Spinlove, oversees an experiment with some Year 8 students at St Helena School in 2002.

Other Year 8 students look on eagerly as a fellow pupil gets to grips with another experiment.

In this view from June 1911, children from the town's elementary schools are assembled on the Recreation Ground to celebrate the Coronation of King George V. Note the party dresses and elaborate hats worn by many of the pupils and their teachers.

From the early years of the 20th century science had become an increasingly important subject in the curriculum of most secondary schools, as pupils were being prepared for life in the new age of technology. These pictures from East Ward School in 1947 show a large well equipped Science Room where various experiments involving electricity and magnetism can be practiced by the pupils. Here a young pupil is examining the interior of a valve radio set which he has helped to assemble.

The handicraft room at East Ward School in 1947. Each boy at the school would have spent approximately 10 percent of his learning hours working in this room being taught the rudiments of both wood and metal working, in order to fulfil a curriculum which gave fairly high prominence to manual subjects. The lower picture shows some of the achievements of the students following a relatively short period of instruction.

Two very contrasting views of the same classroom at St John's Green School. The older picture, with the rising tiers of desks, is from the early 1930s and shows a typical classroom arrangement of the period. The picture shows there to be at least 50 children in the class, and the circular emblems seen across the rear wall may have represented the four different school house systems, a feature which still survives in the modern set up. The lower picture shows the same classroom as it appears today with a much less formal structure and far more decoration on the walls.

Young pupils from the class depicted above engage in a period of quite concentration as they settle down to their studies.

What a difference 37 years makes. Many of the young pupils seen here lining up for a class photograph at St Ann's School in 1957 were pleased to re-assemble for a grand reunion in Colchester Town Hall in 1994. The reunion was for those pupils who had later attended East Ward School in the early 1960s.

Chapter 3
Transport

Throughout the 19th century and the years leading up to World War One, the roadways of England were very much the domain of the horse. Nearly all forms of transport were horse-drawn and by the turn of the 20th century, the number of horses being used in this capacity had exceeded three million. The kind of vehicles in use was varied, ranging from small private traps and gigs to larger commercial wagons and omnibuses.

One type of carriage however which was popular in towns and cities throughout the country, including Colchester, was the horse-drawn hackney carriage. This, of course, was the forerunner of the modern taxi and, in the days before the advent of the electric tramway and other forms of motorised transport, it was the most popular form of public transport. The carriages came in all shapes and sizes, but were generally classified as being either two- or four-wheelers. The most popular four-wheeled carriage in Colchester during the late Victorian and Edwardian period was a vehicle known as a brougham.

This could accommodate up to four people seated in a small enclosed carriage and was drawn by a single horse. The most popular two-wheeler at this juncture was without doubt the hansom, a lighter more racy type of vehicle which was particularly favoured by the younger members of society. The hansom was also reckoned to be somewhat faster that than the ordinary four-wheelers, despite the fact that all hackney carriages were supposed to conform to a maximum speed limit of just six miles per hour.

The opening of the town's new tramway system in July 1904 heralded in something of a revolution in local transport. For the first time an affordable and convenient system of transport had been made available for the masses, and for just one penny a person could travel from the centre of town to either North Station, Lexden, Harwich Road or the Hythe. The trams began their daily service at six in the morning, continuing throughout the day until 11.30 at night. They were all open-top double-deckers which meant avoiding the upper floors, if at all possible, during bad weather. Unfortunately, the tramway network was fairly limited in its scope and by the late

1920s had been abandoned in favour of a new motor bus service.

The most remarkable innovation in road transport during this period, however, was the motor car and even more astonishing was the speed at which it all took place. From most traffic still being horse-drawn at the dawn of the 20th century, by the outbreak of World War One the streets were becoming filled with motor vehicles.

The car, of course, was to give people a freedom of movement never before realised, despite being given a definite 'thumbs down' in the early years by many of the town's older inhabitants. This, of course, was a view shared by the ageing Queen Victoria who had vividly expressed her dislike of 'this newfangled contraption' in a letter to the Duke of Portland. The Queen wrote, 'I hope you will never allow any of these horrible machines to be used in my stables. I am told they smell exceedingly nasty and are very shaky'.

In fact, an Act of Parliament in 1865 had severely hampered the development of the motor car with the introduction of very strict speed limits, and the controversial red flag law. The Act forbade speeds in excess of 4 mph (2 mph in built up areas) and required each vehicle to be accompanied by three attendants, one of whom was to walk 60 yards ahead of the car carrying a red flag. This law was finally relaxed in 1896 and the speed limit raised to 12 mph.

The early motor cars were little more than horse carriages which had been fitted with an engine, and standards of engineering were generally quite poor resulting in innumerable problems for the would-be motorist. The first car to arrive in Colchester is believed to have been that owned by Arthur Stopes, manager of the Colchester Brewing Company on East Hill. The year was 1896 and it must have caused some excitement as the car chugged its way up and down East Hill.

By 1914 many of the earlier engineering problems had been sorted out, and with an estimated two million cars already in use worldwide, the scene was set for what was to become one of the most popular inventions of all time.

A charming late Victorian studio photograph showing three young boys astride a tricycle. Although far removed from our modern highly sophisticated machines, the invention of the early bicycle, and indeed tricycle, was of tremendous social importance providing an independent means of transport for those who could afford nothing else.

A penny-farthing race from the 1880s. The exact location is not known.

A late Victorian photograph showing an unknown lady seated in a phaeton carriage outside the former Paxman's Social Club on Hythe Hill. The phaeton was especially designed for personal use and became widely accepted as a lady's carriage. Some models, however, including the one depicted incorporated a groom's seat at the rear where the carriage could also be driven by a coachman in livery.

A solitary brougham horse-cab waits for a customer in this late 19th-century picture of the High Street. The cab would have been one of more than a hundred similar vehicles licensed by the council to ply their trade on the streets of Colchester. A journey in a horse-cab would have cost anything between 6d (2½p) and 1s (5p) a mile which was a little beyond the reach of most folk for use on a regular basis.

The line of horse-drawn vehicles seen here descending Balkerne Hill in the early 1900s are probably taking part in some kind of official celebration such as the annual Co-op or St George's Day parade. Horse-drawn vehicles such as these were a common sight in the early years of the 20th century delivering all manner of goods around the streets of Colchester and beyond. In fact, many were still being used for such work up to the late 1940s.

This view shows a large horse-brake standing outside Farmer's cutlery shop in the High Street about 1910. Such vehicles were popular for group outings in the years before World War One, and this group are probably about to set off on a pub outing, or some similar activity. The combined weight of both cart and passengers could obviously have proved a burden for the horses which is one of the reasons why those on board would have been expected to get off and walk up any hills.

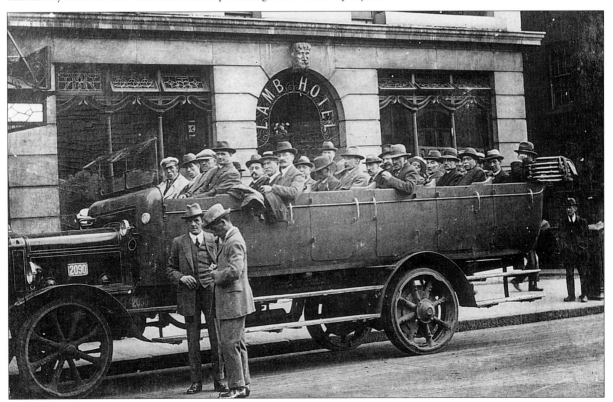

By the 1920s, the horse-brake had largely given over to the motor charabanc, which provided a little more in the way of speed and comfort. In the scene depicted, a group of 25 or so men are about to leave on a trip from outside the Lamb Hotel in the High Street.

By the 1930s and '40s group travel arrangements had moved on apace with fully enclosed motor buses having taking over from the open-topped charabancs. In this photograph from the mid-1940s workers from St Leonard's Laundry at the Hythe can be seen preparing to embark upon a day trip to Southend. At least two buses were needed to accommodate the 50 or so strong workforce.

This modern coach interior shows just how far group travel arrangements have progressed from the days of horse-drawn carriages and open topped motor charabancs. Luxurious seating and on-board air conditioning are now standard features on many modern coaches. The group depicted are all members of the Friends of Colchester Museums en route for an evening visit to Maldon.

On 28 July 1904 the opening of Colchester's new tramway heralded in a new age of cheap transport for the masses. The initial fleet of 16 open-topped double-deckers operated on routes to Lexden, the Hythe, East Gates and North Station. Passengers could obviously avoid the exposed upper decks during periods of bad weather and seek shelter down below, but not so the drivers who were particularly exposed to the elements.

The tramway route to East Gates was the first to close in November 1927 in preparation for major road improvements and bridge widening at East Bridge. The tram rails were not re-laid and in May the following year the route was taken over by motor buses.

This view shows Crouch Street looking west towards Lexden in 1904. The approaching tram is en route to North Station and the street appears quite busy with people going about their everyday business. Note also the evidence of recent horse traffic activity, and the early motor car seen parked alongside the buildings on the left.

The former Recreation Hotel building still dominates this busy junction near Old Heath and Military Roads despite the passing of 90 or so years between these photographs. The Recreation Ground was as far as the trams went on this section of track before being driven back in the opposite direction to North Station. Apart from the solitary approaching tram seen in the top picture, the road appears to be fairly quiet as evidenced by the two young ladies posing for the photograph to the left of the tram.

The end of an era. Tramcar No 13 stands rotting in a field after having trundled through the streets of Colchester for more than 25 years. And of the initial fleet of 16 trams which began operating back in July 1904, this was very same tramcar which headed the procession and carried the mayor and mayoress on the first official journey.

Tram rails being removed at the top of Queen Street in 1954.

This view of the High Street looking east in 1905 typifies the Edwardian era. Carrier carts, horses and a tram combine to add to the atmosphere. The photograph would appear to have been taken on a Saturday as evidenced by the small market stall seen to the right of the picture, below the temporary sign above J. Sainsbury's new store.

Above: An assortment of early motor buses line up in the former St John's Street bus station in 1926 en route for such destinations as Halstead, Tiptree, Chelmsford, Maldon and Braintree. *Below:* The same scene in 1975 after the site had been converted into a car park.

Although Colchester never had its own motor bus service until the demise of the tramway system in the late 1920s, other bus companies had been operating in the town since before World War One. The vehicle depicted was typical of the period having evolved from the horse-drawn carrier and omnibus trade.

This busy scene from the mid-1930s shows more buses lined up at the St John's Street bus station. Note the double-decker at the end of the row with its covered upper storey.

Following the closure of the bus station in St John's Street in 1961, a new site was opened at the top of East Hill which was later refurbished to incorporate a multi-story concrete car park.

The bus station as it appears today minus the car park which survived less than 25 years.

A corporation bus on route to Middleborough via the High Street and North Hill in the early 1950s. This particular model could carry 52 passengers and was the first of the diesel-engined buses in Colchester. Note the cover over the radiator grill in an attempt to provide a little warmth in the interior.

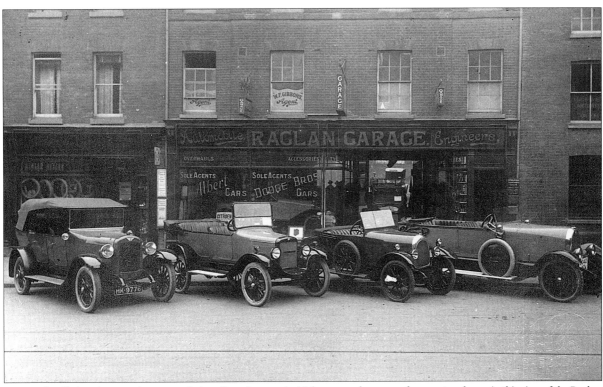

One can hardly imagine a modern garage being allowed to use the highway as a showroom forecourt as shown in this view of the Raglan Garage in Head Street sometime around 1920. A car like one of those depicted would probably have cost something between £200-£300.

Members of the Colchester Motor Club seen outside Metcalf's garage in the High Street in the early 1920s. Note the sign in the shop window advertising for sale a new Super BSA motorcycle for £65. A similar machine today would cost anything from £5,000.

Culver Street has changed almost beyond recognition over the years as this photograph from the 1930s clearly shows. The view is seen from a position near the present day Bank Passage and is looking towards the narrow entrance into Head Street. In fact, the only building which has survived, in part, to the present day is the façade of the old Bunting Gymnasium which is depicted here as the gabled building on the right. Note the 1930s-style motor cars parked in the road which were probably among the latest models of the day.

This view shows part of the Culver Street car park in the 1960s. The site was cleared a decade or so later and incorporated into the new Culver Shopping Precinct.

Chapter 4
Occupation & Trade

By the mid-nineteenth century, Colchester like many provincial towns of its size was developing industrially and emerging as an important centre for small-scale engineering, boot and shoe manufacturing and wholesale tailoring, to name but a few of the town's industries.

The largest of the engineering firms was the Standard Ironworks on Hythe Hill, originally founded by James Paxman and brothers Henry and Charles Davey in 1865. The firm steadily expanded from fairly modest beginnings employing just a handful of men, to becoming the town's largest single employer of labour with a workforce of more than 2,500 in the 1960s.

The firm specialised in the production of steam engines and boilers, many of which were exported to such far away places as South Africa, Russia, China and Japan. In 1904, Standard Ironworks supplied the engines to power the town's new tramway system and, in the same year, produced its first internal combustion engine. By the 1940s, they were producing engines for all classes of marine, rail traction and stationery work, and during World War Two supplied over 4,000 engines for use by the Admiralty to propel British landing craft in virtually every allied assault operation.

In the second half of the 19th century, from around the time of the Crimean War, the town also enjoyed a thriving boot and shoe industry. The trade particularly flourished from around the 1860s when some of the more enterprising firms decided to take on larger premises and install new machinery to increase output. They also took advantage of the expanding railway network which enabled them to seek customers over a far wider area. The trade developed to such an extent that, by the 1890s, it was poised to overtake engineering as the town's main business activity. The industry's largest employer at this time was an Irishman named John Kavanagh, who began trading in the town as a clothier and outfitter in Magdalen Street, before turning his attention to the repair and resale of discarded army boots. He was soon to be employing a workforce of nearly 400 after securing lucrative contracts with the military involving the annual repair of some 100,000 army boots. Added to this, his factory was producing an annual total of nearly 200,000 boots and shoes of every description. By the turn of the 20th century, other leading firms in the industry were Knopp & Son of Portland Road, who employed over 100 men, A.C. George who employed a similar number at his factory in Kendall Road and numerous other smaller firms employing a few dozen each. Within a few years, however, the bubble had burst and the industry had fallen into decline. Kavanagh's closed down completely and many of the other factories and workshops were adapted for other use.

Kavanagh's factory had, in fact, been taken over by the large London clothing firm of Hollington Brothers who, after carrying out a complete refit of the building, were soon employing a staff of over 200. For the wholesale tailoring industry was another of the town's Victorian success stories. One of the first involved in the trade locally was without doubt Hyam Hyam, a Jewish pawnbroker and second hand clothes dealer who had set up shop in St Botolph's Street in 1817. He was later to become a pioneer of the ready-made clothing trade and, in particular, the practice of sub-dividing the labour process among poorly paid female workers.

And despite being criticised from several quarters, including the male tailoring trade, both he and his several sons went on to become major players in the ready-made tailoring industry opening up premises in several of Britain's major cities. Back in Colchester, Hyam and several other tailoring houses, had ensured that the trade flourished for well over a hundred years providing employment for thousands of local women, both in the central factories and as outworkers in their own homes. For reasons, however, that have still not been fully explained, this industry also fell into decline from the around the 1950s, and within another 20 or so years had largely come to an end.

Water Board contractors prepare to lower a section of 27in diameter water main beneath the railway line at North Station in 1956. The new main was part of an ambitious project to link the large storage reservoir at Great Horkesley with the rest of the supply network in Colchester. Before the system was brought on line, however, inspectors had to crawl through the entire two mile or so length of pipework to check that all the joints were satisfactory.

With the steam engine and carriages having safely passed through the station, workmen can now begin to lower the pipe into position. Note the Town Hall and Jumbo the Victorian water tower looming on the horizon.

This view shows a gang of workers from the Water Board laying a new main in the Prettygate area in the 1950s. Note the small mechanical digger at the end of the trench and the use of ropes to lower the heavy pipe into place.

The modern method of pipe-laying would appear to be much more straightforward. On this occasion, at a building site in Elmstead Road, Phil Leeper and Shayne Johnston merely guide the six metre long seamless length of pipe into place as it is lifted up by digger driver Brian Peacock.

A group photograph of the Colchester Borough Police Force in 1901. Every person pictured is sporting a moustache and several are also wearing either military or service medals. Chief Superintendent H.G. Ackers can be seen wearing a peaked cap and holding a cane in the centre of the group, which are assembled on the lawn of Holly Trees House. Note also the rather nondescript looking 'police dog' lying on the rug.

This view shows the mounted section of the Colchester Borough Police Force outside the castle in 1910. The section is led by Sergeant Wynn and is being reviewed by the Chief Constable Mr S.R. Midgley. The police force at this time did not have their own horses, but would hire them when needed from the local cavalry barracks.

This before and after photograph of the local traffic police shows that it is not only the cars which have changed their appearance. The top picture, which dates from the early 1950s, was taken at the rear of the old police station in Queen Street (now the Chicago Rock Café). From the left are Taffy Bateman, (unknown), Bill Littlewood, Bert Takely, Fred Hagen, Norman Plummer and Bill Geddis. The lower picture shows PCs Trevor Sleet and Steve Woods standing alongside their modern Vauxhall Omegas at the Colchester Traffic Unit's current base at Stanway.

PC Freddie Brooks of Colchester Borough Police on his Triumph motorcycle in the 1930s.

Culver Street looking west from a position near the old library in 1940. The building on the right is the printing works of Benham & Co Ltd, a firm which has been trading in the town since 1846.

The office staff of Benham & Co Ltd about 1960.

Hervey Benham, grandson of the founder of the business, shares a moment with two young compositors at the Culver Street works in the late 1950s.

The machine room at the Culver Street works around 1940 when the *Essex County Standard* was being produced on an old Wharfedale flatbed printing press.

What a contrast between the old compositors' room at Benham's Culver Street works in the 1930s, and the modern set up at the firm's new factory on Severalls Industrial Estate. Whereas in the past, up to 20 staff may have been required to prepare the typeface for an edition of a local newspaper, the same type of work can now be undertaken by a single operative. In this picture, Dave Cookson can be seen preparing a computerised image for the page of a modern telephone directory.

Most of the work currently carried out by Benham & Co Ltd revolves around the production of telephone directories. In this view, taken in the firm's new factory extension at Severalls Industrial Estate, technicians can be seen making final adjustments to a new bindery unit which will be capable of dealing with up to 15,000 telephone directories an hour.

Line supervisor, Martin Hunt, checks that everything is okay as fully bound telephone directions roll off the production line in January 2002.

A rare group photograph showing the postmen of Colchester in the early 1920s. Note the long service badges being worn by several of the men pictured.

One of Colchester's serving postmen during the 1920s was Arthur Warne, seen here in his rather military style uniform.

The uniform may have been toned down a little, but our modern-day postmen, seen here represented by John Bright, continue to provide a much valued service to the local community.

One of the last horse-drawn corporation dust carts pictured in Osbourne Street in 1935.

By 1938 a new corporation depot had been opened at Jarmin Road, complete with a fleet of modern vehicles.

In this view from 1956, foundry workers at Paxman's engineering company are seen pouring molten metal into a mould as part of the process of producing an engine part. In fact, the picture could have been taken anytime over the previous 70 or so years as the foundry area changed very little over time. The man seen on the left of the picture is George Adams. Today's health and safety officials would be appalled at the lack of protective equipment for the men.

This view of Paxman's foundry was taken in 1946 and shows a number of moulds in which cylinder blocks are due to be cast.

The Test Shop at Paxman's in the early 1960s. Many of the diesel engines produced by the firm were destined for use on the railways, either in the form of a separate locomotive, or as concealed engines fitted below individual carriages. Engines used for this latter type of installation had to be quite flat in design, in the same style as the first two engines depicted in this illustration.

This picture shows part of a diesel engine assembly line at Paxman's in the 1960s. The man seen at the bottom of the picture is fitting the bearing shells; the next man is fitting the crankshaft; and the next man, after the engine has been turned upright, is fitting the cylinder blocks. Such a form of production was considered quite innovative at the time but it was not to last. Today all the engines produced by the company are assembled in one location.

In this picture from Paxman's factory in the 1950s, the man in the foreground is operating a turret lathe. This type of machine has only recently been finally phased out in favour of more modern computer-controlled units.

A modern multiplex machine centre of a type which has replaced the old type lathe. The machine can be used for a number of milling, drilling and turning operations quite independently of the operator who, after setting up the controls, can observe from a safe distance. In this illustration the man setting the controls is Alan Littlewood.

A slightly faded but rare photograph of the original workforce of Maurice Wood's Electrical Engineering firm. The business was started in a small workshop at the Hythe in 1909 and has over the years developed into what is today the town's largest industrial outlet with a workforce of more than 600. The company is currently one of the market leaders in the manufacture and supply of electrical fans supplying a worldwide market.

This picture shows two employees working on a motor housing for one of the fans in the early 1950s.

Another picture from the 1950s showing two young Wood's apprentices busy fixing tags to an electrical motor.

There was a time, of course, when the employment of apprentices was a natural progression in most areas of industry. In this view from 1956, Wood's training officer Alf Jackson is seen instructing a group of first year apprentices. Until comparatively recent times, the company would regularly take on about 10 new trainees each year to begin a comprehensive five-year apprenticeship.

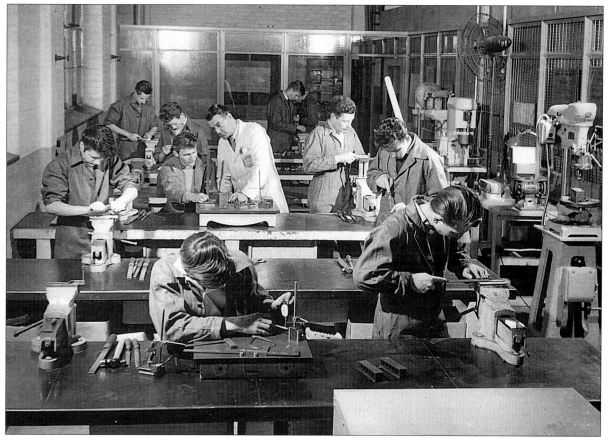

These two views, showing assembly workers at Wood's factory, were taken about 40 years apart and show that very little has changed in this side of the operation. In the top picture, which dates from about 1960, the man on the right can be seen lowering a motor into a fan housing with the aid of an electrical pulley. In the lower picture, Peter Stephens, right, can be seen carrying out the same operation, while his colleague, Barry Mitchell, is working on a fan housing.

The very mention of the name Gunton in Colchester will usually conjure up images and, indeed, the aroma of freshly roasting coffee. The firm, which was established in the 1930s by Herbert Gunton, is still very much a family concern with Herbert's grandson Keith currently in charge of things. In this picture, Geoffrey Gunton, son of the founder, can be seen measuring out some freshly roasted coffee beans at the Crouch Street shop in the early 1970s.

Despite his advancing years, Geoffrey Gunton still attends the shop on most days of the week to supervise the roasting of the coffee beans.

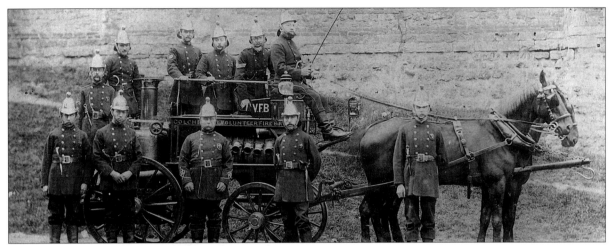

Colchester Volunteer Fire Brigade pictured outside the castle in 1880. The brigade was one of two fire fighting forces in the town, the other being operated by the Essex and Suffolk Fire Insurance Society. By the end of the 19th century, however, both of these brigades had been disbanded and replaced with an official fire service run by Colchester Borough Council.

Colchester Corporation Fire Brigade at their Stanwell Street depot about 1900. Note the vertically mounted steam boiler which would have driven the water pump. The boiler itself would have taken some time to fire up and produce steam, not to mention the time required in preparing and harnessing the horses to pull the engine. Only then would they have been in a position to attempt to fight the fire. The horse-drawn engine was finally replaced with a motor driven vehicle in 1921.

Members of Green Watch pictured alongside their fire rescue tender at Colchester Fire Station in 2002.

A firemen braves the billowing smoke as he tackles the blaze at Kent Blaxill's High Street store in 1952. In total, 11 fire crews from across north-east Essex battled with the blaze for three hours before bringing it under control.

Smoke billows from the Woolworth's store in the High Street during the fire which destroyed the premises in 1973.

A Colchester Borough fire engine from 1935. Note the fairly basic escape ladder attached to the vehicle and the fact that there is no covering whatsoever to protect the driver or crew from the elements.

This view shows the rear of the present fire station building as it appeared in September 1938 at the time of its opening. Note the assortment of rescue vehicles including fire engines and ambulance equipment.

These two photographs recall a popular image from the past. Before the arrival of the modern supermarket and the advent of the milk carton, most people looked forward to the early morning arrival of the milkman with their daily 'pinta'. The top picture shows a horse-drawn milk cart owned by W.J. Watts of Military Road about 1920, complete with large metal churns for carrying the milk. The lower picture shows Albert Hewitt with his Co-operative Society hand cart sometime in the 1930s. Albert joined the Co-op as a milk roundsman in 1928 when a bottle of milk cost 3d (1p).

This picture shows a group of tailoresses busy working at their sewing machines in Hollington's clothing factory in the early 1930s. Colchester had for many years been a thriving centre of the ready-made tailoring trade providing employment for thousands of local women, both as factory hands and out-workers alike. The garments which they produced were entirely in the form of men's clothing, largely for the export market. Note the hats and coats hanging ready to hand on the rear wall.

A rare photograph of Fred Brackett and three of his staff at his Hythe Station Road factory sometime between the wars. Pictured from the left are: Fred Brackett (managing director), W. Callaghan (turner), Bob Warboys (fitter) and Fred Petitt (fitter). Fred Brackett was just 27 when he founded the firm of F.W. Brackett & Co Ltd in 1899. The firm was to later specialise in the manufacture of filtration equipment for power stations and other large installations.

A large drum screen occupies much of the floor area in this view of Brackett's factory at Severalls Industrial Estate in the 1980s.

George Bellman (right) oversees the loading of a hub and shaft assembly for a drum screen outside the machine shop at F.W. Brackett's Hythe Engineering Works in the late 1960s. It was also about this time that the firm was taken over by the famous Hawker Siddley Group and subsequently relocated to the Severalls Industrial Estate. Today the company is known as Brackett Green and forms part of the giant Belgian Groupe Fabricom.

This row of drum screens, manufactured by Brackett's of Colchester, are pictured shortly after their installation at Hinkley Point Power Station, Somerset in the late 1960s.

Kitchener's Army arriving in Colchester during the early years of World War One. The smiling faces and seemingly casual nature of those pictured is a world apart from what was to come on the hostile battlefields of northern France and Belgium.

An interesting view of the Gordon Highlanders about to embark upon a train at St Botolph's station. Note the outline of St Botolph's Church and Hollington's clothing factory on the skyline.

Colchester camp, *c.*1890 showing the original wooden huts erected at the time of the Crimean War. The town has enjoyed a large military presence ever since, although the old wooden huts had all been replaced with brick buildings by the early 1900s. The current military population in the town amounts to about 5,000, made up of serving soldiers and their families.

A modern view of the barracks looking towards Mersea Road.

The Essex County Hospital
medical staff in 1902.

The Essex County Hospital
nursing staff in 1902.

Nursing staff on Gainsborough
Ward at Colchester District
General Hospital in 2001.

This interesting group are all outpatients at the Essex County Hospital in 1902. Note the straw hats and long skirts worn by several of the women and the Norfolk jackets and high starch collars worn by some of the boys. In fact, despite their attendance at a hospital outpatients unit, they look to be a pretty healthy group of individuals.

This picture shows staff members of the Colchester Union Workhouse about 1918. The young girl seen in the centre of the group is thought to be Marjory Collins who was the daughter of the Master of the House.

Chapter 5
Leisure, People & Events

This chapter takes a look at some of ways in which we used spend our leisure time, and indeed, in many cases, continue to do so. We will also be taking a closer look at one or two local personalities. Certainly during the period before the advent of radio and television most people were happy to make their own entertainment spending much of the leisure time away from the home.

In the early years of the 20th century one of the most popular entertainment venues in Colchester was the Hippodrome Variety Theatre, which is where most of the leading vaudeville stars of the day would come to perform. These would have included such stars as the singer Marie Lloyd, Vester Tilley, Harry Champion, George Formby (senior) and the comedian Charlie Chaplin before he emigrated to America. The house used put on three shows daily – a matinée performance in the afternoon and two more in the evening, the latter of which were nearly always full often resulting in long queues to get in. During one matinée performance in June 1906 the audience got a little more variety than they had expected. Midway through the performance a large bullock came striding into the auditorium and stood staring at the audience and glancing towards the stage.

Fortunately, before anything too untoward could occur some drovers came rushing in and persuaded the animal to leave the building.

By 1910 the first of the town's picture houses had opened in St John's Street near Headgate Corner. It was named the Electric Theatre (later the Cameo) and was screening films continuously throughout the day from 2.30pm to 11pm. In later years, this was also the first cinema in the town to screen 'talking pictures'. In the following year the Vaudeville (later the Empire) opened in Mersea Road which was the first made purpose-built cinema in Colchester. In 1920 the Hippodrome theatre also became a cinema and by the 1930s, these three houses had been joined by the Playhouse and the Regal making five picture houses in town all showing the latest films.

In addition to the regular entertainment provided at the cinema and theatre, there were often numerous outdoor events taking place, such as a travelling circus or funfair. One of the most spectacular events of this kind to have performed in Colchester was Buffalo Bill's Wild West Show which arrived in the town in September 1903. Buffalo Bill and his large entourage, which included several hundred horses and performers, arrived early at North Station on three specially hired trains. Thousands of onlookers lined the streets as the performers, which included Sioux indians, Plains cowboys, Russian Cossacks and Mexican vaqueros, all mounted on beautiful horses, made their way to the showground at Reed Hall. By midday a spacious arena had been erected with undercover seating for 10,000 spectators. In the afternoon the town almost came to standstill as crowds flocked to see the show. Many schools were forced to give a half-day holiday due to the wide absenteeism. The whole performance was repeated in the evening before the entire camp was dismantled, loaded back on to the trains, and the show en route to its next venue.

The church also took a leading role in the provision of many forms of entertainment. Most churches, for instance, supported groups of boy scouts and girl guides and various other social groups for young people. For older members of the congregation there was the Mothers' Union or Women's Institute for the ladies, and perhaps a supper club for the men.

On a secular level the network of social groups was even greater. Most public houses and large places of employment supported their own football or darts team, as well as taking an active interest in cricket, cycling and athletics. In 1907, the founding of the Colchester Social Clubs League provided yet another outlet for those interested in playing competitive cards, cribbage and draughts. The league was made up of 10 teams of 12 players. At competitive meetings three team members each played draughts and cribbage, whilst the remainder played whist. Points were awarded for each game won and, at the end of the season, the team which had accumulated the most points was adjudged the winner and presented with the Lord Cowdray Shield.

The 14th Colchester Girl Guides pictured in the grounds of Christ Church in 1932. All the girls in the group were pupils at the County High School for Girls, including Nora Frost who can be seen in the third row from the front, second from the right. Note the full length navy blue dresses and the wide-brimmed hats.

By the early 1960s the dress code for guides had undergone something of a transformation. In this picture of the 14th Colchester Girl Guides dating from the early 1960s, it can be seen that the full length dress has given way to a skirt and blouse, and the wide-brimmed hat to a beret. Also by this time, Nora Frost had risen up the guiding ranks to become Captain of the Company and can be seen here in the centre of the gathering wearing the dark coloured uniform.

Members of the 1st Myland (35th Colchester) Scout group pictured at the Thorrington camp site in 1961. The lad having his hiking equipment inspected by Brain Mead, the camp warden, is Patrol Leader Bob Russell who in 1997 was elected MP for Colchester. He was mayor in 1986-7 and has served as borough councilor from 1971 to the present day. The other Scouts are Swift Patrol members Peter Spurgeon (left) and Peter Rash.

Colchester Scouting in Parliament. Pictured with the Speaker of the House of Commons, the Rt Hon Betty Boothroyd MP, at the 2000 Scout Association's Annual Parliamentary Tea Reception held in Speaker's House, are long-serving Colchester Scout supporters Ivan and Joan Russell (no relation to Bob), Scouts Rachel Wallace and Bella Shah and Colchester MP Bob Russell who is secretary of the All-Party Parliamentary Scout Group. In his youth (see above) Bob was a Queen's Scout and gained the Duke of Edinburgh's Gold Award.

1st Boxted Scout Troop assembled for church parade in the late 1930s. Note the regulation short trousers and wide-brimmed hats being worn by the boys, a requirement which has long since been relaxed.

1st Myland (35th Colchester) Scout Group pictured in 1991. The group, which was formed in 1956, has a current membership of some 40 individuals made up of beaver scouts, cub scouts and group leaders. When this particular photograph was taken the leader of the group was Mick Brown who can be seen seated in the centre of gathering.

Successful swimming competitors line up for a group photograph following the opening of the new open-air pool in Colne Bank Avenue in June 1932.

The open-air swimming pool in Colne Bank Avenue was a major attraction in the town before its closure in 1972. It was the next best thing to being at the seaside and many people will have fond memories of hot sunny days spent lounging by the poolside.

Members of the Colchester Bowling Club line up for a group photograph after winning the Buckingham Hospital Cup against a team from Severalls in 1924. Pictured from the left are: Councilor F.W. Richards, Mr Buckingham, Mr Ray and Mr Russell.

A rare action photograph of a mixed doubles tennis match from the early years of the 20th century. The long dresses worn by the female competitors provide some clue as to the age of the picture, as do the flamboyant hats and clothing worn by the spectators in the background.

This line up of local and national dignitaries are assembled to inspect the archaeological excavation work at Lion Walk in July 1972. The work was being carried out by the Colchester Archaeological Trust under the leadership of site director Philip Crummy. Pictured from the left are Alderman L.E. Dansie, Bernard Mason, W.E. Buckingham (mayor), Philip Crummy, Sir Mortimer Wheeler, Major J.G.S. Brinson, unknown, Peter Holbert, Len Drinkell, Len Gant and Rex Hull.

Thirty years later and with scores of further archaeological digs behind them, the Colchester Archaeological Trust is still as active as ever. In this picture from July 2001, members of the excavation team line up for a group photograph at the former St Mary's Hospital site.

Philip Crummy (Colchester Archaeological Trust) and Anne-Marie Bojko (Colchester Museums Service) examine the remains of a Roman skillet (pan) found in a grave at Stanway.

Since its official opening in 1892, the Castle Park has continued to provide a welcome retreat for those wishing to escape the hustle and bustle of the town centre. The top view shows several children and a few adults walking in the park to the north of the castle near the entrance to the Dutch Quarter. The lower view shows young and old visitors alike relaxing by the Roman style fishpond in the late 1920s.

This view of the Castle Park was taken shortly after it opened to the public in 1892 and shows a group of workmen busy tending the lawns and shrubberies. The initial landscaping of the park had been completed by a firm from Yorkshire whose brief was to create a parkland landscape rather than a formal municipal garden. Today the park contains over 500 trees and 5,000 shrubs.

This recent view of the Castle Park shows that apart from the obvious maturity reached by a number of trees, very little has changed in the general layout of the area. Note also the beacon to the left of the picture which was erected in 1988 as part of the 400th anniversary celebrations of the defeat of the Spanish Armada.

An archery contest under way in Colchester during the 1920s, possibly at the Garrison Officers' Club.

Lady Judy Buck, wife of our former Member of Parliament Sir Anthony Buck, delivers a pep talk to members of the local archery team at the British Team selection trials in 1986.

Bill Tucker (right), founder member of the Colchester and District Archery Club, is presented with a native bow from Kenya by Lord Alport in about 1960.

Members of the Essex Archaeological Society on a visit Colchester in 1922. The gentleman pictured near the centre of the group with walking stick in hand is the late Sir Gurney Benham.

Regulars of the William IV pub in Artillery Street line up for a group photograph in the early 1900s. The sign above the door names the landlord as Henry Smith and would suggest that he was also a dealer in fish and fruit. His customers would appear to be taking part in some kind of celebration given their reasonably smart appearance. Or perhaps they have just returned from church!

A scene from the Colchester carnival of 1938. The float pictured belongs to Fred Martin's outfitting shop in St Botolph's Street and the line of girls standing to the right are advertising the St Botolph's Street Traders Association.

During the 1930s, a number of girls from Hollington's clothing factory did their own little bit each year to help brighten up the carnival by dressing up as soldiers. They paraded in proper uniforms, which had been made at the factory, complete with wooden rifles at their sides.

Although such a scene would doubtless be frowned upon in some quarters today, the Edwardian public liked nothing better than turning out to greet the arrival of a travelling circus. This view shows a herd of elephants passing along Crouch Street towards the town centre in the early 1900s.

Another scene which would certainly be frowned upon by today's public. A dancing bear and its handler are seen in what is believed to be Lexden Road around the turn of the last century.

The sign on the building in the background of this photograph identifies the location of this meeting of the local hunt sometime in the 1930s. It is of course the Leather Bottle public house near the junction with Shrub End Road and Gosbecks Road.

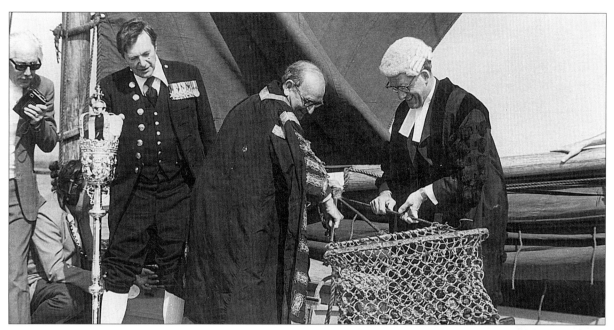

The Mayor of Colchester Councilor Bill Ladbrook and John Allen, town clerk, haul aboard the first oyster catch of the 1975 season. Holding the mace is Jim Spong the town serjeant and recording the event for local hospital radio, with tape recorder in hand is Bill Tucker.

Invited guests (all male) assemble in the Corn Exchange to celebrate the Oyster Feast in October 1896. The mayor on this occasion, and host of the gathering, was Councilor James Wicks, leader of the Liberal Party. Although the exact origin of the event is not known, the earliest record of the feast appears in Chamberlain's accounts for 1667 where we read that '2 hole barrells and 4 halfs of oysters were sent up by Mr Mayor's orders' at a cost to the town of 16 shillings (80p).

Both male and female guests can be seen at this Oyster Feast gathering in October 1978. The event is taking place in the Moot Hall and the mayor at the time was Councilor David Holt who can be seen seated third from the left in the lower left corner.

The Theatre Royal in Queen Street as seen in around 1900. At the time this was the principal place of entertainment in Colchester where locals would flock to enjoy a drama, musical or pantomime. The theatre had been built in 1812 with seating for over a thousand, although from the early 1900s its popularity had began to wane as a result of a new variety theatre opening in the High Street. Its final demise came in 1918 when the building was destroyed by fire.

The aftermath of the fire at the Theatre Royal in 1918. Firemen can be seen surveying the damage which was too great to consider rebuilding.

Before the days of modern-style rock groups, most musical entertainment was supplied by dance bands such as the one depicted here. The band was called the Black Diamonds and was led by Bunny Burnham who is seen seated at the drums. The picture is believed to have been taken at the Co-op Hall in the 1930s when the group was playing one of their Saturday night gigs.

Veteran broadcaster Bill Tucker is seen here interviewing Robin Day at the 1976 Oyster Feast. Recording the interview for Radio Colchester are Chris Dowsett (left) and Paul Diggens.

A proud moment. Bill Tucker pictured at Buckingham Palace with his wife Betty and daughter Gillian after receiving his MBE. The award was given in recognition for Bill's involvement in a wide range of services to the community.

These two strikingly similar views of the Mayor's Parlour in the Town Hall were taken nearly 100 years apart. The top picture dates from 1904 and shows the then mayor, Councilor Ernest Barritt, sitting at his desk. In the lower picture, taken in 2002, the mayor, Councilor Mike Hogg, is seen occupying the same position.

A rare photograph of staff and inmates at the Colchester Union Workhouse taken around 1918.

The former workhouse as it appeared in the early 1990s. The building was erected in 1836–7 following the Poor Law Amendment Act of 1834 which required parishes to form together into large unions. The house opened in 1837 and operated continuously under an elected Board of Guardians until 1929 when its responsibilities were transferred to the local authorities. In 1938, the former workhouse was renamed St Mary's Hospital.

Another extremely rare photograph showing a group of female inmates at the Colchester Union Workhouse in the early 1900s. Note the shift dresses being worn with drawstrings for tying around the neck and waist and the black armband worn by the lady in the middle row, perhaps indicating a recent bereavement.

These children from St Mary's Infant School are standing in front of the Roman wall for this group photograph c.1920. Several young children from the nearby workhouse are known to have attended the school during this period, and at least two of the girls in the picture appear to be wearing traditional workhouse style clothing (back row, third from left and middle row, far right).

The Colchester Wanderers – Teddy Grimes and Marmalde Emma – two well known tramps who roamed the local highways and byways in the early years of the 20th century. Although the couple were never married they were inseparable and apart from a few nights spent in the workhouse, where they had to endure separation, they rarely left each other's side. Emma finally succumbed to a severe bout of bronchitis in 1917 and died in a lodging house in Vineyard Street aged 58 years. Finding life difficult without his former companion, Grimes soon entered the workhouse where he lived out his final years before himself dying at the age of 65 in 1924.

Index